The end of our freedom?

Agenda 2030 & the great reset exposed!

Hyperinflation – Economic Crisis – Future
Globalization

Truth Leaks Books

Disclaimer

Cashless society?

Introduction of global biometric payment system now actually underway *- Pay with Face: Brazil first country where you can pay with your smile - WEF works towards digital 'Beast' system by 2025*

For years we have been writing that cash will be eliminated in the future and replaced by a fully digital global payment system. Since 2020, the signs that this system will be introduced in the near future - such as the announcement of the arrival of a Central Bank Digital Currency (CBDC), which, according to the CEO of Mastercard, could replace the SWIFT payment system in 5 years - have been getting stronger and stronger. Some time ago, we wrote that the European Union is working toward having cash eliminated by the end of 2023. In Brazil, Mastercard has now started a pilot project with a biometric payment system that will soon be rolled out all over the world: Pay With Face.

As usual, the latest 'surveillance capitalism' initiative is being sold as something that will make life even easier. 'No more fumbling with your phone, or having to look for your wallet when your hands are full' (well, what an insurmountable drama that would be, imagine!). 'The next step in personal payments needs only a brief smile or a movement of your hand.'

The same technology that already allows you to unlock your smartphone with your face or fingerprint can now be used by consumers to pay for their purchases with lightning speed. With MasterCard's new Biometric Checkout Program, "everything you need is yourself.

Three quarters of consumers would be positive

Globally, 74% of consumers would be positive about the adoption of biometric technology. 4 out of 5 already use some form of contactless payment with their bank card. In most countries, people would therefore be eager to exchange their PIN for, for example, their fingerprint, which can be used to make a payment via a special sensor on their card.

This eliminates the need to touch a PIN device or a fingerprint device, and all people have to do is smile into a camera or move their hand over a sensor. It's not hard to imagine that yet another "contagious virus" could be used as an argument to get people to embrace this contactless tech.

Paying with your smile in Brazil

The first pilot project kicks off this week in Brazil with the installation of the company's Payface technology in 5 St. Marche supermarkets in São Paulo. Customers who register with the Payface app will be able to pay with their smile only in the future. Future pilots are planned in the Middle East and Africa. After that, it will presumably be the turn of the rest of the world.

In addition to Biometric Checkout, Mastercard has other innovations being tested to make payments easier, such as Shop Anywhere. The company has been developing secure methods to verify people's identities using their bodies instead of a password or (PIN) code for some time.

While Mastercard, which sees itself as a global leader towards a 'World Beyond Cash', always emphasizes that consumers retain control over how their personal data is shared, the many data leaks from mega-corporations such as Facebook and government agencies such as the Dutch Tax Administration do not exactly inspire much confidence in that promised 'security'.

Collaboration with Bill Gates leads to global vax passport

Bill Gates' GAVI vaccine alliance partnered with Mastercard and Trust Stamp, an "ID authentication" company, in 2020. The program was first launched in late 2018, integrating Trust Stamp's A.I.-powered ID platform with the GAVI-Mastercard 'Wellness Pass,' a digital vaccine ID system connected to Mastercard's Click-to Play system, which is based on self-learning A.I. technology ('Nudata').

Mastercard's collaboration with Bill Gates' GAVI alliance brings the introduction of a comprehensive global biometric ID system, which will be directly linked to your future mandatory vaccination 'passport' and your bank account, very close. Called "The Wellness Program," this collaboration was piloted in West Africa in 2020.

Trust Stamp's biometric ID system, funded by Mastercard, uses a technology called Evergreen Hash. This creates a '3D mask' generated by an A.I. based on a person's face, palm or fingerprint. This 'hash' can be updated every time, such as when you've received a new vaccine.

If this - or a similar - system is soon rolled out worldwide, it will be possible to check the whereabouts of every person who is linked to it 24/7/365, and of course whether this man, woman or child has had their latest mandatory vaccine injected.

Flashback to 2020: Microsoft patent 060606

In April 2020, we reported on Microsoft patent application 2020-060606 for a technology that links the human body directly to a digital payment system. Bill Gates' "old" company Microsoft developed a system with a "device" (nanochip?) that works directly with the human body's temperature, heart rate and brain waves to buy and sell (with) a digital currency.

This system determines, based on your body, whether you meet certain 'conditions' to be allowed to buy or sell. It is not difficult to imagine that among those conditions is a mandatory vaccine, which has digital markers (such as nanobots) in it that can be detected and/or read by the chip.

In addition, the system could theoretically signal not only you but also the authorities if your body temperature rises. You could then receive a call to report to a doctor or hospital as soon as possible, where you would be checked for the presence of a virus or other illness.

Flashback to 2009: Sign of the Beast introduced via mandatory vaccinations?

We have cited this famous Bible passage many times over the past few years in various articles about these end times:

"And the (beast) makes, that to all, the small and the great, the rich and the poor, the free and the slaves, a mark be given on (older translations: IN) their right hand* or on their foreheads, [and] that no one can buy or sell, but he who has the mark, the name of the beast, or the number of his name (666). (Rev.113:16) * The word translated 'hand' at that time also referred to the complete arm up to the shoulders.

Already on September 24, 2009, so almost 13 years ago, we wrote in our article 'Will the Sign of the Beast be introduced through vaccinations?' that 'it (is) conceivable that the "Sign of the Beast," which according to the Bible will be introduced in the final phase of human history, will consist of vaccinations containing ingredients that will change our human DNA, and which will be administered after a planned outbreak of a deliberately constructed deadly virus.'

'Does the 'Sign of the Beast' perhaps also have a literal meaning? That the people who are injected with partly human, partly synthetic, partly animal gene-altering substances are no longer fully human after their vaccination, but partly 'beast'? Would that be part of the reason why Revelations says that no salvation is possible for these people even during their lifetime?'

It is not difficult to imagine that during the worldwide panic and chaos that will be caused by the outbreak of a deadly pandemic, the coming 'Antichrist system' will be able to quite easily give 'everyone, both big and small' the 'sign'...

In this scenario it would also make sense that anyone who does not receive the 'sign' will no longer be able to 'buy or sell', as such unvaccinated people may be forcibly quarantined to prevent the spread of the virus. Thus, in this respect too, the prophecy of the 'sign of the Beast' would be fully fulfilled.

WEF works toward digital 'Beast' system by 2025

The recent WEF report Advancing Towards Digital Agency (February 2022) almost literally announced a digital 'sign of the Beast' system (see our article on this). Every human being is to have a 'data intermediary', a kind of digital 'middleman' or 'copy' of yourself. In fact, it comes down to the fact that you will get a government-controlled personal digital 'god' who will make all important decisions for you, because that 'god'

(= so the government) would know, based on all your personal data, exactly what you want and need, and when and where.

Your' digital ID will really be linked to EVERYTHING: healthcare, insurance, financial services, bank accounts, food and sustainability, travel and mobility (= passport, buying tickets), humanitarian response ('to access services and show qualifications to work abroad'), E-commerce (to store and pay online), social platforms, E-government (including voting, which means that elections will go digital and the outcome can therefore no longer be trusted) and all forms of telecommunications.

Under the heading 'Future' there is literally talk of the 'next level of data intermediaries ('embedded in your body' = embedded in your body, devices, houses, cities, etc.)'. Of course, these include the 'vaccine passports' no one wanted: 'These passports naturally serve as a form of digital identity.'

Remember that in 2019 it was decided to accelerate this transhuman agenda, which was initially supposed to be realized by 2030, to 2025 ('The Accelerator'). This was most likely done because the global awakening that we are dealing with the darkest, most anti-human and downright diabolical system ever here is happening faster than what the WEF globalists had taken into account.

So the WEF, in cooperation with NATO, the EU and the US, is making every effort to have the "System of the Beast" completed by 2025, or at least well advanced in its implementation. Given the frightening geopolitical developments, it is certainly not inconceivable that 2025 will be brought even further forward (2023-2024) by means of a number of major wars - planned or unplanned - (Ukraine-NATO/Russia, China/Taiwan, Israel/Iran, India/Pakistan), financial-economic crashes and major disruptions in the energy and food supply.

Table of Contents

British bishop: Putin only world leader to stand up to Power of Evil - *Russia destroys US missile transport for Ukraine - NATO exposed as paper tiger as army defeats Ukraine in just 3 months - 'Possible coup against Zelensky as he lost Donbass'*

A secret summit meeting took place in Lithuania yesterday where plans were drawn up for the 'Deputinization' of Russia. German reporter Julian Röpcke attended the summit, and reported that the participants were betting on a deadly 'accident' of Vladimir Putin. This is nothing less than the disguised announcement of an assassination attempt on the Russian president. As a reminder, the immediate cause for the outbreak of World War I was the assassination of Archduke Franz Ferdinand in Sarajevo in 1914.

The brazen anti-Russian lying propaganda and hate speech in the West is taking increasingly absurd forms. For example, British Prime Minister Boris Johnson imitated the illustrious Winston Churchill by comparing Putin to a crocodile: 'How can one deal with a crocodile, which is about to eat your left foot? What can you negotiate about then? And that's what Putin is doing.' Johnson therefore seems to be fully committed to a 'hot' war between NATO and Russia, once again calling for the potential total destruction of his country.

Putin only leader to stand up to Power of Evil'

On the contrary, unexpected support for the Russian leader is coming from British religious quarters. British Bishop Richard Williamson, in a sermon in Warsaw, actually called for Putin to be supported because he is the last obstacle to the establishment of a New World Order (led by WHO, WEF and US/EU/NATO):

'Of the heads of government, only one has stood against the Power of Evil. It is not Boris Johnson in England. It is not Macron in France. It's not Draghi in Italy. It is Vladimir Putin. He may not be an angel or a saint, but he is nevertheless a smart man of great courage. And as the head of state of Russia, he has the ability to oppose the One World Government.

Williamson stressed that Putin did not invade Ukraine to divide and destroy it, but to de-nazify and demilitarize it. Russia was forced to defend itself, he continued. The real aggressor is not the party that seemed so at first glance (the Kremlin), but is in Kiev, which has been supported in this by the West since 2014. 'Stupid Europe is following the orders of the US in its attempt to crush Russia,' Bishop said.

Ukrainian army indeed defeated; NATO put on display

As we wrote a few weeks ago, the Ukrainian army has indeed been defeated. All the while, the Western media and politicians spouted false propaganda that the opposite was the case, that Ukraine was winning.

The fascist President Zelensky, glorified in the West -
who is utterly unscrupulous in using child soldiers and
against whom a coup may be launched for losing the
Donbass - could not help but admit that "the reality
must be faced" that his army has lost. Foreign Minister
Kubela has therefore been instructed to start
negotiating with Russia after all to end the war. Former
President Petro Poroshenko, meanwhile, is said to have
tried to flee the country, for which he was arrested near
the border with Poland.

The demise of the heavily demotivated Ukrainian army
in just 3 months is especially painful for NATO, as it
financed, trained and armed these soldiers. The
Western alliance has been exposed worldwide as a
paper tiger that can't actually do anything.

Last Sunday, for the first time, the Russian military
carried out a direct attack on a large-scale U.S. arms
shipment for Ukraine. Kalibr cruise missiles destroyed
near the Malin station (Zhytomyr region) a load of
missiles and other weapons supplied by the US and
European countries.

'Russia will not leave Ukraine until victory is achieved'

Dimitry Peskov, a Kremlin spokesman, reiterated that
Russia will not withdraw troops from Ukraine until all
goals are accomplished and victory is achieved. Noted
NWO top man Henry Kissinger suggested that Ukraine
then just surrender some areas to Russia, since mostly
Russian-speaking people live there anyway.

In essence, Kissinger advocated nothing more than implementing the Minsk agreements ignored by the US/EU/NATO/Kiev. If those had been adhered to, this war would never have broken out.

Is Russia blocking grain shipments, or...?

In retaliation for the unjust and rock-hard Western sanctions, some 20 Russian warships would block Ukraine's Black Sea ports, preventing some 22 million grains from being exported to at least 36 countries. Egypt, Lebanon, Qatar, Pakistan, Indonesia, Jordan, Malaysia, Thailand and parts of Africa would potentially be threatened with famine as a result. One proposal is for this blockade to be broken by Western naval forces, but that would mean immediate direct war with Russia.

It is conceivable that the report on this Russian blockade has been manipulated, as it comes from the Israeli DEBKAfile, which always stands squarely behind the United States and has proven to be far from an objective source on the war in Ukraine.

Monkey pox planned? NTI scenario from 2021 assumes 3.2 billion infections and 271 million deaths by 2023

'Monkey pox vrius appears to have been manipulated to be resistant to vaccines' - *Or is this a pretext to cover up the huge number of Covid-19 vax deaths?*

Corona/Covid appeared to have been planned and prepared from A to Z, which was proven fairly soon after the outbreak of the so-called 'pandemic' in 2020. It seems that it may well be the same story with monkeypox. Indeed, in March 2021, the Nuclear Threat Initiative (NTI) partnered with the Munich Security Conference in drawing up plans to mitigate dangerous biological threats. One scenario assumed an "attack" with the monkey pox virus on May 15, 2022 (or 5 days ago), followed by a small-scale outbreak on June 5 for which no warnings or advisories are yet issued internationally. With fatal consequences: by December 1, 3.2 billion people have been infected and 271 million have died.

The fictional 'Brinia' is, in the NTI/MSC scenario, 'ground zero' of a new pandemic that has been announced several times by Bill Gates (see our earlier article today). Initially, there are only 1421 infections and 4 deaths in 'Brinia', so the international community sees no reason to take action.

However, by January 10, 2023, the monkey pox has reached 83 countries. 70 million people are infected, and the death toll has risen to 1.3 million. Scientists discover that the virus has been manipulated in a laboratory to be resistant to all vaccines. International supply chains come under great strain from the pandemic.

3.2 billion infections and 273 million deaths

Just four months later, on May 10, 2023, the number of infections has exploded to 480 million, and the number of deaths to 27 million. Authorities reveal that a terror group managed to infiltrate a civilian laboratory, obtaining the engineered virus.

(Which is also quite plausible that the huge number of Covid-19 vaccine deaths will be attributed to this new deadly virus, IF it exists at all. We have discussed this scenario regularly since 2020.)

By the end of that year, the situation is dramatic. On December 1, 2023, 3.2 billion people are infected, more than one-third of the world's total population. 271 million people have died. Globally, there are great differences in approaches to the pandemic, which also means that there are very different outcomes. The NTI, in its 2021 paper "Strengthening Global Systems to Prevent and Respond to High-Consequence Biological Threats," therefore called for "more funding to be prepared for pandemics," exactly mimicking Bill "vaccine" Gates.

New infections and new vaccines purchased

Australia, Canada, Italy and Sweden have now reported
their first monkeypox infection(s), as have the US,
Spain, France and Portugal. On May 6, the first infection
outside of Africa was detected in the UK. It involved a
man who had been in Nigeria and is believed to have
contracted the virus there. Meanwhile, there are a total
of 9 confirmed cases in the UK.

Meanwhile, U.S. authorities have once again stocked up
on a hefty dose of "vaccines" against the monkey pox
virus. The Biomedical Advanced Research and
Development Authority (BARDA) last Wednesday struck
a $119 million deal with Danish pharmaceutical
company Bavarian Nordic to supply millions more
injections in 2023 and 2024.

We reported that the federal government stockpiled
large quantities of smallpox vaccines as early as 2013,
when the disease was supposed to have been
eradicated for quite some time. In September 2021, the
Biden administration purchased $112.5 million of the
drug TOPXX, which was developed to treat smallpox.

Whether this is a real modified virus, or a pretext to
cover up the huge masses of Covid deathvax victims,
does not matter at the end of the line. What is certain is
that gigantic numbers of casualties are expected in the
coming years, and that those deaths will occur because

a global elite club, led in part by the WHO and WEF, so desired and planned.

Bill Gates in interview 2021: 'What if a bioterrorist releases smallpox at 10 airports?'

'Monkey pox may have reached Manhattan, New York' - Flashback to our November 25, 2021 article: 'US government poised to release 'Angel of Death' smallpox virus announced by Gates' - Monkey pox virus: Gates' second pandemic or another scare hoax?

11.35 - 'What if a bioterrorist releases smallpox at 10 airports?' Did Bill Gates use this question during a Policy Exchange interview in 2021 to let people know that the next p(l)andemic was already being prepared? Did he initiate this p(l)andemic now? In the meantime, in fact, the "monkey pox" has also reached Manhattan, New York. Are we awaiting, sooner than expected, a new era with strict lockdowns, mouth masks, and this time probably also mandatory vaccinations for everyone and the forced quarantine of huge masses of people?

On November 25, 2021, we wrote in our article "U.S. government is poised to release 'Angel of Death' smallpox virus announced by Gates that the billionaire eugenicist is 'patently trying to instill new fears, not only to extract additional billions to 'vaccinate' the entire world population over and over again, but also as an additional argument for handing over even more power to the UN and WHO's Special Pandemic Task Force (= thus to him).'

On November 7, 2021, we reported that Bill Gates has ordered the West to put tens of billions into preparations (lett. 'Germ Games') for the next p(l)andemic. 'These 'germ-games' that Gates is talking about sound like false flag exercises to unleash 'germs' (pathogens) on the world, and come at a time when we know that the globalists in their sick minds feel it necessary to wipe out a large portion of the world's population,' All News Pipeline concluded.

'If the first pandemic doesn't convince you...'

Gates announced in 2020, with a gaudy grin, that 'if the first pandemic doesn't convince you' (to have you inject 'vaccines' with gene manipulation), then the second will.' During 2021, he suggested that the next pandemic might be with the Marburg virus, but not long after, he changed that to a return of the dreaded smallpox.

Smallpox would have been eradicated by 1980. So why in September did the Biden administration slam the drug TOPXX, developed to treat smallpox, for $112.5 million? Incidentally, the federal government was already striking down large quantities of smallpox vaccines in 2013. In the fall of 2021, all of a sudden, peculiar "smallpox" reports appeared in the mainstream media. An employee of a lab in Philadelphia - which pharma giant Merck owns - allegedly just stumbled upon 15 medicine bottles containing the smallpox virus in a refrigerator somewhere.

Then Bill Gates came out with the warning that 'terrorists' (was he looking in the mirror at the time?) are planning to release a smallpox bio-weapon, and governments should therefore spend billions (on 'vaccines', of course) to prevent 'future pandemics'.

'So after the pandemic 'exercise' Event201 (in October 2019) with the outbreak of a coronavirus became a reality just 3 months later, the next planned pandemic - whether with smallpox, a modified Marburg virus, or some other (whether or not it really exists) 'killer' - could soon 'go viral' around the world,' we wrote on November 25, 2021.

Another, equally plausible explanation is that governments should be able to pinpoint some kind of 'false flag virus' as soon as millions of people become seriously ill and/or die from the Covid injections, an extremely frightening but by numerous experts predicted development whose evidence continues to accumulate since last year in the form of an explosion of serious heart disease, blood clots/thrombosis, immune disorders, organ problems and a huge list of other serious side effects, which have officially killed more than 44. 000 people, and have permanently damaged the health of millions.

The survivors of the coming pandemic, if it were up to Gates (and thus the WHO = the real global government) should all get a 'vaccine patch' in your arm, which may well be the completion of the foretold pricked 'sign of the Beast', which all vaxxers are now incrementally integrating with.

Monkey pox - second pandemic or another fear hoax?

Now that the monkey pox virus has possibly reached Manhattan, New York, after Canada, the United Kingdom, Portugal, Spain, Italy and Sweden, the question can be asked whether Gates' announced pandemic has now actually begun. In Quebec, Canada, 13 suspected cases are already under investigation. In Europe, the virus, whose danger is currently downplayed, is said to be spreading mainly among gay and bisexual men.

According to Dr. Amesh Adalja, infectious disease expert at Johns Hopkins University in Baltimore, the virus spreads through physical touch. Only people who already have symptoms (fever, headache, rash that starts on the face and spreads all over your body) spread it through aerosols (exhaled mini droplets in the air).

However, it is also possible that the "monkey pox" narrative is just meant to keep the people scared, so that they don't ask too many questions about the totally failed, for many fatal Covid "vaccinations", and of course to prepare them for Gates' real two planemic, which will be used to justify handing over all national competences to the WHO, which will function as a kind of de facto world government.

Nuclear threats?

US Stratcom admiral warns nuclear deterrent is in crisis

A.I. Socrates: Escalation in 2023, but world war probably not until after 2024 - *Swiss president prepares people to 'use nukes in this war' - Ukraine blames 'Russian occupier' for shutting off gas to Europe*

US Stratcom Admiral Charles Richard declared to Congress yesterday that a 'crisis in nuclear deterrence' has emerged. Nuclear weapons are no longer the great barrier that keeps superpowers from entering into indirect or even direct armed conflict with each other. This has created an unprecedentedly dangerous situation in the world. Great Britain has already decided to add more nuclear warheads to its arsenal of Trident missiles, and France has three of its four nuclear submarines permanently at sea for the first time in 30 years, compared to only one normally (7). A growing number of analysts therefore fear that a world war will break out within a few years in which nuclear weapons will actually be deployed.

'We are currently facing a deterrence crisis that we have only seen a few times before in the history of our country,' Richard said. 'The war in Ukraine and China's nuclear trajectory - their strategic breakout - shows that we have a breach in our deterrence and certainty in terms of the threat of limited nuclear (weapons) use.'

He also warned that 'China is closely following the war in Ukraine, and is likely to use nuclear coercion for their own benefit in the future. It is their goal to acquire the military capabilities to reunite Taiwan by 2027, if not sooner.'

Nuclear weapons have lost deterrence; Signature West is no longer worth anything

So nuclear weapons are no longer a sure deterrent. They have never really been able to maintain world peace anyway; just look at the many wars fought after WW2. The fact that Russia is the other major super nuclear power did not stop the US/NATO/EU from undermining Ukraine, taking over de facto and making it a military 'base', severely oppressing the Russian-speaking minority, and thus provoking a Kremlin military intervention.

In the process, the Minsk Accords signed by all parties are completely ignored by both Western politics and mainstream media. And why? Because if those accords - which, among other things, provided for free elections for the residents of the Donbass - had simply been observed, nothing would have happened and war would not have erupted. Mentioning those agreements would alert people to the fact that Western signatures and promises are worth zero point zero, and thus the US/EU/NATO power bloc has become totally unreliable.

'WW3 more likely after 2024'

Top American economist Martin Armstrong has often pointed out that his unique A.I. 'Socrates' has never made a wrong geopolitical prediction in decades. Therefore, he is certain that China is going to overtake the U.S., just as it has already overtaken Europe.

'After they got Biden appointed, tensions started to rise. We will see an escalation in early 2023 ('eventually the West will create some kind of false flag to escalate the war and perhaps deploy US troops' (5)), but the prospect of a world war is more likely after 2024. I wonder more if Putin will still be there then than Biden. Putin will be succeeded by hardliners, because they are well aware that this proxy war is in reality a war between the U.S. and Russia.'

Kiev blames 'Russian occupier' for stopping gas to Europe

Ukrainian President Volodymyr Zelensky plays a major role in causing that fatal WW3. Time and again he pleads for more financial and military support from the West. And he's getting it; President Biden has asked Congress for a whopping $33 billion in aid to Ukraine; only $3 billion is for food and humanitarian programs to help the civilian population and 5 million refugees. $20 billion goes directly to the military so it can continue to fight Russia.

The Zelensky regime, meanwhile, blames the "Russian occupying forces" for cutting off the transit of Russian natural gas to Europe. However, Gazprom is fulfilling all its obligations. Therefore, it looks very much as if Kiev is trying to pressure Europe in this way to become even more active in the war, and to provide even more financial and military support.

'Putin is not exaggerating when he says that the West is the aggressor, just as he says that Ukraine is the "accelerator."' The press portrays Putin as a madman who wants to wage war. But his goal was clear from the start: to secure the country he believes belongs to Russia. He has no intention of provoking NATO countries or causing a global disaster.'

'A war the likes of which we have never seen before'

'The US and other (mainly Western) countries have unofficially declared economic war on Russia. We are a few missteps away from an all-out war the likes of which we have never experienced before. Zelensky wants other countries to get involved and join the war, even if it means the loss of millions of lives.

'A war like we have never experienced before' is certainly not an exaggeration. The director of Rocosmos, the Russian space agency, warned that Russia is capable of destroying NATO with nuclear weapons in 30 minutes. 'But we should not allow that to happen, because the consequences of exchanging nuclear attacks will affect the state of our Earth. Therefore, we must defeat this economically and militarily powerful enemy by conventional military means.

Swiss President Ignazio Cassis, however, was already preparing the people for the very worst, declaring yesterday that "in the event of an escalation of this war, there is the possibility of atomic bombs. The Federal Council is also preparing for this.'

Pushing the next world war?

Russian forces today used precision strikes with Kalibr cruise missiles to destroy at least 10 military targets in Ukraine, including a missile factory.

Kremlin and Russian people realize that World War III has actually already begun - 2023 the predicted year when the great devastation begins?

British Defense Minister Ben Wallace has lined up squarely behind Foreign Minister Liz Truss' statement that the Russians must be driven out of all of Ukraine - including Crimea - with military force. This will do nothing less than unleash World War III, a war that the Kremlin and the Russian people are convinced has in fact already begun. It therefore looks very much as if 2023 will indeed be the year in which the great devastation (planned by the US/EU/NATO/WEF complex) will begin. 'Indeed' because 2023 is the possible 'end time' year that we have been predicting for years in articles on this topic.

Wallace and Truss want to start delivering heavy weapons - including tanks and aircraft - to Ukraine. Indeed, a 'victory' over Russia in Ukraine would be of 'decisive strategic' importance. 'We have shown Russia what we are prepared to do,' Truss said.

By now it will be clear to anyone who has not been taken in by the propaganda of Western media and politics that 'our' politicians are not at all interested in a peaceful resolution of the conflict in Ukraine. 'The people at the helm in the West are completely insane,' writes the American top economist Martin Armstrong. 'They seem to think that they can actually destroy Russia, depose Putin, and the Russian people will then somehow welcome this as a liberation.'

Russia convinces that WW3 has already begun

The day before yesterday, Russian President Vladimir Putin threatened "lightning fast attacks" with "all instruments" - including secret ones that the West would not yet know about - once external powers (the West) directly intervene militarily in Ukraine (3). Throughout Russia, especially since the sinking of the flagship Moskva, most likely caused by a NATO missile, there is a belief that World War III has already begun.

In Poland, too, all sobriety and common sense has been jettisoned. Indeed, Climate Minister Anna Moskwa believes that the EU should fine countries that pay for Russian gas in rubles - as, for example, Hungary does. Her bizarre demand was in response to the Kremlin's decision to turn off the gas tap to Poland and Bulgaria because of their refusal to settle in rubles.

Poland pretends to be very altruistic, but meanwhile is simply building a border wall to stop Ukrainian refugees. Some refugees say they get less money than in their home countries, and return.

Europe can't do without Russian energy

The notion in the West that Putin would lose any sleep over the fact that Europe refuses to buy his natural gas is absurd. Russian revenues from fossil energy have actually increased, thanks to skyrocketing prices, rather than declining, as Brussels intended. Therefore, the only ones hurting are us - the ordinary European citizens, millions of whom are now unable to pay the exploding energy, fuel, and food prices, if at all.

Because, according to Finance Minister Lindner, this would be "at the expense of the German people," the German government quickly backtracked on its announcement not to buy any more Russian gas. The country is 34% dependent on Russian energy.

Austria, too, has already announced that it will not ban imports of Russian gas because it cannot afford to do so. The WEF regime has of course already announced that by the end of this year all Russian energy imports must be stopped. (And you know who will have to pay the price for that: you and me.)

Corrupt Zelensky fully supported by the West

Meanwhile, the West, and certainly the Netherlands, continues to support the corrupt Ukrainian neo-Nazi fascist Zelensky unabatedly. No one is talking about the fact that Zelensky. who demands over $7 billion in aid every month, has siphoned off over $800 million for himself to foreign accounts. By the way, the IMF has been complaining about the massive corruption in Ukraine since 2016.

Also, we read nothing here about the serious war crimes committed by the Ukrainian military on the front lines. In the past 24 hours, Ukrainian shelling of towns and villages in the Donbass killed 7 civilians (including a child), and wounded nearly 60 (including 5 children) (9).

'Zelensky agent of Putin'

On the Telegram channel Vedomstvo, Zelensky is cynically derided as an "agent of Putin" because he:

1) Knows how to milk the West financially and pockets some of it himself;

2) Has allowed almost all of Russia's major foreign competitors to leave the country, providing great new opportunities for Russia's own business community;

3) Has Western weapons immediately destroyed by Russia upon arrival in Ukraine, so much so that German Chancellor Scholz acknowledged that the Bundeswehr "no longer has any weapons of its own.

4) Throw all of Europe back to the Middle Ages if indeed we no longer want to buy Russian gas;

5) Ruins ordinary Europeans because of Western sanctions policies;

6) Lured European neo-Nazis, extremists, murderers
and other maniacs en masse to Ukraine to be
slaughtered by the Russian military;

7) Getting the Russian people to back Putin even more
massively;

8) Made the corrupt Ukrainian elite flee the country;

9) Strengthened the Russian ruble;

10) Left the Donbass to the Russians.

Western commentators: 'Putin may well win'

Last week Russia conducted a successful test of the new
ICBM 'Sarmat, a new nuclear warning to the West.
Russian missiles destroyed hangars and depots filled
with American and European weapons in the
Zaprizhzhia region this week. The Kremlin has often
warned that such arms deliveries are legitimate military
targets (5). According to the Pentagon, Russia has
already fired nearly 2,000 missiles (mostly launched
from aircraft) at Ukrainian targets (10).

Amidst the huge load of propaganda and fake news in
the Western media, something of realism and truth is
finally beginning to seep through - albeit gritfully. Here
and there, serious commentaries are being written that
acknowledge that "Putin may well win in Ukraine. U.S.
Secretary of State Anthony Blinken even stated that
"Washington will respect Ukraine's decision to reach an

agreement with Russia on rejecting NATO membership to end the conflict.

Two other countries, Sweden and Finland, seem just about to apply for NATO membership in mid-May. At the same time, Norway has decided to step up its military exercises in the north, where it directly borders Russia.

2023

Armstrong, based on his "never failing" A.I. Socrates, thinks that World War III is likely to break out as early as 2023, and that the West is entirely to blame. The Great Reset, he believes, is going to fail totally. 'In 2022-2023, according to our models, we are going to have panic cycles all over the world the likes of which have not been seen since the 1930s.'

Already several years ago, based on the complete end-time line revealed to the prophet Daniel, we mentioned the year 2023 as a possible year of "the end," and/or the start of the final phase of the end times. The prophecy embraces a period of 1260+1260+35+45 = 2595 years (one prophetic 'day' = 1 year), and counting from the time Daniel received it, comes out quite accurately in 2023. However, a second set of prophecies about the same events ends in 2042, so there is still some slack.

The year 2023, by the way, does not seem to pass without some very drastic calamities. That could include the following violent events:

* A shortage of fertilizer due to the cessation of fossil energy, combined with anti-Russian sanctions and the implementation of WEF policies in the West, will lead to a global famine in 2022 - 2024;

* David Mauriello, a top scientist at the Climate Science Center in Pagosa Springs, Colorado, popularly known as the Oppenheimer Ranch Project, warned last year that our planet may be hit by a devastating super solar flare as early as 2023.

* Scott McIntosh, solar scientist at the National Center for Atmospheric Research (NCAR) in the US, expects a "Termination Event" on the sun possibly as early as 2023, which could have serious consequences for the entire planet.

US drones over Ukraine armed with chemical and biological weapons

Military intervention near? Polish president says border with Ukraine will be erased; British Prime Minister Johnson says 'military aid is no longer enough' - Russians prepare for outbreak of World War III with these 3 scenarios - Putin: 'Unacceptable that NATO is hunting for our territory'

Polish President Andrzej Duda announced a common future for Poland and Ukraine in a speech. 'There will be no more borders between our countries, no more border between Poland and Ukraine. So that we will live together on this earth, building and rebuilding our common happiness and our common strength, which will enable us to repel any danger or any potential threat.' Meanwhile, U.S. drones equipped with biological and chemical weapons would be deployed over Ukraine.

Ukraine's fascist leader, Volodymyr Zelensky, recently called again for more Polish military support for his country. If the borders are indeed removed, Poland could theoretically supply an unlimited amount of weapons to the Ukrainian army.

Poland prepares people for battles with Russian troops

At the same time, Poland will be able to send military units into the country itself, something that has been rumored before and now seems to be confirmed. In fact, the government in Warsaw has begun preparing the people that Polish troops will be deployed in Ukraine, fighting directly against the Russians.

Between May 1 and May 26 week, large-scale military exercises will take place along the border with Ukraine. Those exercises are part of Defender Europe and Swift Response. Some 18,000 military personnel from more than 20 countries are practicing under the command of the 5th U.S. Corps in 8 European countries for the outbreak of a military conflict with Russia.

The statements by President Duda - whose grandfather was a friend of Ukrainian Nazi fascist Stepan Bandera - can actually be understood as a disguised announcement that the territories in western Ukraine could be annexed by Poland, under the guise of helping against the Russian "aggressor.

'US drones with chemical and biological weapons active over Ukraine'

American drones have been sighted over the Kherson region. According to Russian officials, these drones are equipped with biological and chemical weapons, and may already be deployed. This would be a very serious war crime, but that is something the Americans have never cared about.

Russia insists that it got rid of all chemical weapons five years ago. Izumi Nakamitsu, the undersecretary general for UN Disarmament Affairs, says Ukraine does not possess chemical weapons. Yet a top U.S. diplomat testified before the Senate that the "Pentagon is working to ensure that materials from biological research do not fall into the hands of Russian forces.

This suggests that the U.S. laboratories recently discovered in Ukraine did indeed run a secret biological weapons program. However, Zelensky continues to claim that this was "just scientific research," and warned that all countries should fear Russia's use of chemical or nuclear weapons. However, given the facts, it seems more likely that not Russia, but Ukraine possesses chemical weapons.

Russians prepare for outbreak of World War III with these 3 scenarios

Putin's top advisors are therefore warning against a "provocation aimed at accusing the Russian armed forces of using chemical, biological or tactical nuclear weapons," according to Lieutenant General Igor Kirillov.

As NATO countries send more and more financial and military aid to Ukraine, the Russians are preparing for the outbreak of World War III with these three scenarios:

1. An attack on the Zaporozhuskaya nuclear power plant, which is controlled by the Russians. This plant is

in critical condition, according to the Defense Ministry, which could lead to a disaster that Moscow will be blamed for. World leaders could very well use this for a declaration of war.

2. The Pentagon deploys small amounts of weapons of mass destruction, for example, against the large steel plant in Mariupol. This too will be blamed on Russia.

3. The third option is the least likely, and that is the direct use of tactical nuclear weapons on the battlefield. The danger is enormous that this will rapidly degenerate into a global nuclear war.

Boris Johnson wants WW3 that Putin is trying to avoid at all costs

That NATO is out for a "hot war" with Russia is something we have been writing about for many years. That moment is drawing ever closer as British Prime Minister Boris Johnson literally declared yesterday that "military aid to Ukraine is no longer sufficient to defend it. Also, the Trident missiles aboard the British submarines have been equipped with additional nuclear warheads.

All this means that the British want large-scale Western military intervention, which automatically means World War III - a war, by the way, that NATO is going to lose without a chance if nuclear weapons were indeed deployed.

'We are doing everything we can to prevent the horrors of a world war from happening again,' President Putin stressed today at the annual Victory Parade in Moscow, which commemorates the defeat of Nazi Germany. The Russian leader also called it "unacceptable" that "NATO is actively hunting for our territory... We are talking about neo-Nazis in Ukraine, which the U.S. and its partners are cooperating with.

However, Putin held back and did not literally declare war on Ukraine, as observers had expected. Furthermore, the military parade contained remarkably few armored vehicles and other equipment, but a large number of intercontinental ballistic missiles.

Bitcoins and other crypto currencies will be confiscated during upcoming crisis

Amazing how naive most people still are by trusting that the government will abide by its own laws - *The next phase of Great Destruction to enable the Great Reset is at hand*

Crypto currencies like Bitcoin and Ethereum are still presented as a 'hedge' against the skyrocketing devaluation of money and other 'assets'. According to many, it would be the ideal escape that would allow you to keep your digital financial assets out of sight of greedy governments. But is that really the case? We have been writing for several years that crypto currencies actually fit perfectly into the plans to create a new global full digital payment system during the infamous 'Great Reset' crisis, allowing all taxes - and even fines - to be automatically debited from your account. Therefore, nothing will be left of your current crypto wallet after the Great Reset.

Speculating on crypto currencies has already brought many people large profits, but just as many substantial losses. The well-known sales pitch for cryptos - that they function outside the current system - is also wrong for another reason. This is because digital currencies are completely dependent on the government, as they can confiscate all of your bitcoins with the stroke of a pen.

Crypto currencies are therefore not long-term assets, but only temporary means of financial trading.

Especially in light of the seven-mile flattening of civil, land and human rights in the context of the corona pandemic, it is downright naive to think that those in power today will stand idly by while an alternative digital currency defeats the current financial system. Anyone who thinks the government can still be trusted and cares about even one law that is supposed to protect citizens still has no idea what untrustworthy and unscrupulous Moloch he or she is up against.

In case of systemic crisis, forget about anything that depends on electricity

In addition, crypto currencies are dependent on the power grid. If the current manufactured geopolitical and energy crisis gets even worse and there arc indeed massive blackouts, as is now expected for Western countries, how can a digital currency - if not already seized and mandatorily exchanged for the CBDC (Central Bank Digital Currency) at a set rate - survive?

During the many wars the US has fought, power plants, the communications network and the water supply were invariably the first targets. If the US/EU/NATO dares to launch a direct war against Russia and China, our energy and communication systems will be the first installations these countries will attack. Cryptos will not survive that.

So during a systemic crisis, forget everything that depends on the power grid. Those only things that retain historical value outside the current fiat money system are tangible "assets" such as real estate, stocks, valuable (art) objects and precious metals. However, in the event of a complete collapse of society, food is the most valuable (exchange) asset (1). If you are hungry and have the choice between a 50 euro bill, a silver coin or a chocolate bar, you will surely choose the latter.

Why do citizens still trust a lawless government?

And as far as wars are concerned, look at what Vladimir Putin did in Ukraine. He took the largest nuclear power plant in Europe, but did not shut it down. Nor did he attack the water supply and leave civilian communication systems intact. This alone proves that he does not want to conquer Ukraine, but only to defend the Donbass and rid the country of its dangerous fascist leaders - who are revered here as darlings and heroes.

It also underscores how morally deeply sunk the West is with its constant anti-Russian lie propaganda campaigns. Also in this light it is astonishing - not to say disconcerting - how many people still think that on the basis of national laws and international treaties they will remain 'safe' from government action, while from the point of view of the protection of citizens and their established rights it is becoming so patently lawless.

Next phase of Great Destruction is near

Now that monkey pox is supposed to have reached the Netherlands, we are waiting for the next series of severe measures such as new lockdowns, which have been shown not to help at all during the corona pandemic, but to greatly exacerbate problems in all areas. New lockdowns will therefore only promote the 'Great Reset' of Klaus Schwab's World Economic Forum, now hated by many - to which the Rutte government is completely subservient.

In short: the next phase the 'Great Destruction' of our society and economy is getting ever closer. Since the population has been expertly played apart with 'diversity policy' and severely weakened with immune system devastating Covid injections, lockdowns and mandatory mouth masks, a mass awakening and peaceful resistance is unfortunately no longer to be expected.

EVERYTHING will be confiscated, including crypto assets. The housing market will collapse and the banks will fall and be nationalized as a result, putting almost all real estate in government hands - exactly according to the WEF's plans. And even if you are debt free you will not escape the dance, because the government will just impose new taxes (/ forced mortgages) on you because of your property.

Don't be naive, proceed with deliberation and wisdom

These plans and measures have been in the works for decades, and are designed to place everyone in a watertight totalitarian digital control system, where it is definitely over with private property and almost all forms of freedom.

This is what we wrote on December 19, 2021, well before the war in Ukraine: 'Depending on geopolitical developments (Russia/Ukraine, China) and the deliberately created energy crisis, the time frame in which the coming crash will take place varies from a few weeks to a few years. But no matter how short or long it takes, it's going to start in 2022 either way. By 2025, we will no longer recognize our country and continent. ALL of our freedom and much of our prosperity will be gone, and if the vax mortality continues as it is now presumably a substantial part of our population as well. We will by design have been plunged into the very hardest and most inhumane totalitarian dictatorship ever.'

So don't be naive by putting your cards on one 'magic solution' such as cryptos. Realize what kind of adversary you are dealing with - one that has at its disposal numerous means of power, and certainly since 2020 has shown no hesitation in using them against defenseless civilians - even the elderly and children. Therefore, always act with deliberation, prudence, caution and wisdom when you are forced to defend your interests and resist the injustice done to you.

Will there be a new disaster?

The Global Seed Vault on Svalbard (Spitsbergen) houses hundreds of thousands of seeds, but it can still be destroyed by an asteroid impact or a sudden sea level rise.

Robots could build a moon base (or maybe it's already there?)

Scientists at the University of Arizona are proposing the construction of an "ark" on the moon. This ambitious project should secure the survival of millions of species of plants, animals and crops in case Earth is struck by a cataclysmic disaster that wipes out almost all life. One of the possible disasters mentioned is the eruption of a super volcano. Another danger we have discussed many times, certainly in the past year, and that is that our planet loses its protection by the magnetic field and is hit by a devastating solar flare. With that magnetic field rapidly diminishing, the possible construction of that "ark" might not come a moment too soon.

The project, which envisions cryogenically freezing the seeds, spores, sperm and eggs of some 6.7 million species in an 'ark' hidden in caves beneath the moon's surface, is led by researcher Jekan Thanga, and was presented at the IEEE Aerospace Conference.

'Global insurance policy'

This modern 'global insurance policy', which will be powered by solar panels, is going to serve as a DNA repository in case the Earth needs to be repopulated after a cataclysmic disaster.

'Earth is by nature a volatile environment,' said Thanga, professor of aerospace and mechanical engineering at the UArizona College of Engineering. 'For humans, it was about 75,000 years sideways due to the Toba super volcano eruption, which caused a 1,000-year cooling, and some say equated to an estimated decline in human diversity. Because human civilization has such a large footprint, if it collapsed it could have a negative chain reaction on the rest of the planet.'

'I like to use the analogy with data,' he continued. 'It's like copying your photos and documents from your computer onto a separate hard disk, so you have a backup if something goes wrong.' After an apocalyptic event such as a super volcano eruption (like Yellowstone), a nuclear war, an asteroid impact, a pandemic, or a solar flare/storm, survivors can hit a sort of 'reset' button, and begin to rebuild civilization.

Lava tunnels

According to Thanga, the moonark should be built in lava tunnels and caves. Discovered by scientists in 2013, these caves were formed by the drying up of lava channels and pahoehoe (basalt or "smooth" lava) flows. So far, a network of some 200 of these structures has been discovered, which some say are so enormous that a planetary base could be built in them.

These huge 'tunnels' provide protection from external elements (such as impacts from meteorites) and have a temperature of about -25 degrees Celsius. However, to cryogenically preserve the seeds, a temperature of - 180 degrees Celsius is required. An even lower temperature of -196 degrees C. applies to stem cells.

Quantum levitation

To avoid mechanical failure of the cooling equipment needed to do this, Thanga's team proposes using a phenomenon called quantum levitation. This is based on cryo-cooled superconducting material - a material that transfers energy without heat loss - floating above a powerful magnet. The two parts are linked at a fixed distance, so that wherever the magnet goes, the superconductor follows.

'It's like they're attached to each other with invisible wires,' the professor explained. 'With cryogenic temperatures, strange things can happen. Sometimes it just looks like magic, but it's based on tried and tested physics principles in laboratories that border on our ability to understand.'

Quantum levitation could also be used to send flying and jumping miniature robots into the tunnels and have them gather information about their layout, temperature and composition. Such an off-earth task force of robots could also help build the base itself, as well as install the solar panels that would provide the electricity for the cryogenic modules. An elevator is also needed to transport the samples and building materials to the base of the lava tunnel.

Only 250 launches needed

One of the biggest obstacles is how to transport all the samples and necessary goods and materials to the moon once the project is complete. With current technology, it would take about 250 rocket launches to bring 50 samples of each of the 6.7 million species to the moon. 'It took 40 launches to build the International Space Station (ISS). So it's not insanely massive. We were quite a bit surprised about that.'

On Earth, such an 'ark' already exists: the Svalbard seed bank (Global Seed Vault), an installation on the Norwegian archipelago of Spitsbergen, where hundreds of thousands of samples of seeds are stored in case biodiversity is severely reduced or even lost due to, for example, a global disaster. However, this 'Global Seed Vault' can still be destroyed by an asteroid impact or a sharp rise in sea level.

'Beginning space civilization'

Although thorough research needs to be done on how the lower gravity will affect the seeds, and how the ark should be controlled and monitored from Earth, the team is confident that the complex can actually be built on the moon. An "ark" in a large space station around the Earth would be closer, but not safe enough due to unstable orbit.

UArizona doctoral student and thermal specialist Álvara Díaz-Flores Caminero sees the project as humanity's next step toward a "space civilization, and toward a not-too-distant future in which humanity will have bases on the moon and Mars.

Within 30 years, but is that enough?

According to Thanga, the Moon Ark can be built within 30 years. That seems like a long time, but given Earth's rapidly diminishing magnetic field, a pole reversal already underway, and the increasing risk that our planet may be hit by a devastating solar flare/storm as early as the short to medium term, one can seriously question whether there is still enough time for that.

Does a moon base already exist?

It will be familiar to many readers that for decades there have been speculations about the existence of secret bases on the moon. These are said by some to have been built by the Nazis, the Americans, or by extraterrestrials.

That sounds less science fiction than you might think. For example, tests with explosives have shown that the moon appears to have a hollow interior, and the surface of the moon is covered with material that is partly from the interior. This seems to indicate that the moon is being used by a technologically advanced civilization to closely monitor humanity.

Astrophysicists have always been amazed that a comparatively small planet like Earth has such a large moon, and that from the Earth's surface that moon is visually as large as the sun, which is many times further away from our planet. Unique coincidence? Or indeed a strong indication that, there is much more going on with the moon than has been widely publicized.

European Commission wants to monitor all instant messages - on your own device

Direct attack on all confidential communications and basis of freedom of expression - *Even normal pictures and messages will be marked as 'wrong' and forwarded to authorities*

The European Commission has presented a draft law to monitor all chat messages and automatically forward them to the authorities. The A.I. (Artificial Intelligence) based system will check the content of every message and all pictures directly on your own device (PC, smartphone) ('client-side scanning'). Phrases and images identified as 'suspicious' should then be 'redirected'. This planned extreme invasion of our privacy would supposedly be necessary in the fight against child abuse (of which it is known that the elite elite themselves are most guilty, also in the Netherlands).

Victims of child abuse should indeed be much better protected and helped. However, checking chat messages is clearly a highly exaggerated measure whose effectiveness is highly questionable, and which is also easy to circumvent, certainly by criminals.

The real goal of the EC therefore seems clear: to introduce a total digital control and surveillance state, in which there is no more room for free (dissenting) opinions, nor for any privacy.

Direct attack on all confidential communications

The planned draft law foresees that every device will screen for images of child abuse and criminals' contacts with children. If such content is recognized, the messages will be diverted directly to a government agency or the police.

This mass scanning of all your messages is a direct attack on the basis of all confidential communications of ordinary citizens. Criminals already make ample use of all kinds of alternatives and detours (Darknet, encrypted messages) that are not affected by the scans anyway, and will be able to easily circumvent these scans in the future.

Journalists and whistleblowers in particular depend on confidential communication, which is a fundamental right and an important pillar of all IT security. Communication is only confidential if a device does not send private messages to third parties unintentionally, and encrypted messages cannot be cracked.

System will be abused and expanded

European chat control puts these basic fundamental rights out of action. Users lose control over what data they share with whom, and thus lose trust in their own devices.

So far, it is unclear who will create and control the recognition algorithms and databases. Such an opaque system, once implemented, will therefore be very easy to abuse and extend to messages that contradict the official narrative about, for example, the war in Ukraine, Russia, climate/energy policy, immigration or the European Union.

Normal photos and messages will also be marked as 'wrong'.

An 'artificial intelligence' that examines messages for certain illegal content will make the necessary mistakes. Even the smallest 'wrong' quotes, expressions, phrases and perfectly normal photos showing adults and children together will be falsely 'recognized' and sent to the authorities.

Even a very 'good' A.I. system will therefore be confronted with many thousands of messages and photos per day.

Because the assessment of whether certain content should lead to criminal prosecution will (still) have to be done by humans, the already overburdened agencies dealing with child abuse will be even busier.

This will only reduce the likelihood that child traffickers and abusers will be tracked down and caught.

Next step: scanning your thoughts

Governments' technological grip on their subjects will become ever more powerful in the coming years as a new technology is developed in 2020 that will allow your smartphone to be used without your knowledge as a kind of "hub" to access all your other devices, such as car, computer and security system of your home or business, as well as your pacemaker, if any. It can also be used to locate devices belonging to others in your area.

The infamous top man of the WEF, Klaus Schwab, already announced the next step of the global totalitarian surveillance system in the making several years ago. Within 8 years, people who want to cross the border will be given brain scans to determine if they are a potential "danger," and (almost) everyone will be fitted with implanted microchips, which will be required to participate in all aspects of normal life. Even our thoughts and feelings will no longer be our own, and will be able to be controlled and manipulated ('Internet of Bodies').

Gene drive files

***The fertility of humanity and thus our posterity seems
to be in existential danger***

Although the revelation dates back several years, it is
very timely in the context of the Covid mRNA gene
manipulation injections, which have caused untold
damage to the health of millions of people worldwide in
a short period of time: the Gene Drive Files.
Researchers discovered about 6 years ago a load of
emails and other documents showing that the U.S.
military was developing a controversial, powerful new
genetic eradication technology that could also be used
against humans. In addition, the Bill & Melinda Gates
Foundation had put up a substantial amount of money
to get a moratorium at the UN against this dangerous
tech off the table.

Gen Drive technology

Gen Drive technology could theoretically eradicate
nuisance animals such as rats and dangerous insects.
'Gen drives are a genetic adaptation application that
allows genetic engineers to pass a single artificial trait
through an entire population by ensuring that all
offspring of an organism have that trait,' according to
an excerpt from the Gene Drive Files.

As an example, an experiment is given in which mice
were genetically modified so that they would no longer

produce females, but only males. In this way, the population was eradicated after a few generations.

Proponents pointed out that this method could prevent all kinds of infectious diseases and plagues by eradicating their spreaders. However, the emails and documents showed that the development was financed mainly by military funds. This raises the question of whether this tech can eradicate not only parasites, weeds, infectious diseases, dangerous animals and plants, but also humans.

Bill Gates prevents moratorium

In December 2016, UN member states and more than 170 organizations called for a moratorium on these gene drives. However, Bill Gates - eugenicist at heart, who for many years has openly advocated reducing the (growth of the) world's population with the help of "vaccines" - came around the corner, and tried to use his money to make the moratorium go away in the dustbin. He paid the private agricultural and biotech PR firm 'Emerging Ag' $1.6 million to manipulate - in part through a 'coalition' of backers - the UN into not imposing a ban after all.

The emails, revealed after a FOI (=WOB) request by the American Prickly Research, showed that the Pentagon's well-known DARPA (Defense Advance Research Projects Agency) had allocated some $100 million to develop gene drive tech. This involved working with almost all the major players and patent holders of CRISPR gene editing technology. The U.S. intelligence community also showed extreme interest in this.

With the CRISPR/Cas9 method, genomes can be modified by cutting and pasting pieces out of them. However, this tech is not nearly safe or accurate enough; studies have shown that segments of a DNA or RNA molecule with information for encoding, for example, a protein or peptide can be erased, which in the long run can have major consequences for the functioning of the human body.

Tech to eradicate insects has been around for years

In 2016, the prestigious MIT Technology Review wrote that "we have the technology to destroy all Zika mosquitoes in a few months. This technology is called gene drive, has only been applied in the past year in yeast cells, fruit flies, and a species of mosquito that transmits malaria. The tech uses gene-clipping CRISPR method to force a genetic change, which spreads through the population by reproduction.'

Three U.S. laboratories, two in California and one in Virginia, were already working on a gene drive for Aedes Aegypti, the mosquito believed to spread the Zika virus. It was assumed that the tech would be able to eradicate this species of mosquito by inserting - as described above - genetic instructions that would cause these mosquitoes to produce only males.

Gene editing still considered too dangerous for humans in 2020

CRISPR technology, which was first applied to a patient in 2017, was originally developed to be able to combat, and in the future even cure and prevent, hereditary diseases and also cancer.

However, there are necessary caveats to this tech. The Crispr Journal published a paper in 2020 with the views of more than 30 experts regarding the CRISPR gene-editing technology.

Which, contrary to what "Big Pharma," politics and media make it seem, is still controversial in the scientific community because changes made to human genes are passed on to future generations.

In September 2020, an international committee sponsored by the U.S. National Academy of Medicine, the National Academy of Sciences and the British Royal Society concluded that the technology by which genes are edited (gene editing) is therefore not yet ready to be used on humans, because scientists are not yet able to make precise repairs or modifications without causing potentially dangerous changes.

Changes that could, for example, cause autoimmune diseases and cancer.

Fertility at risk?

Why were pregnant women and women who want to become pregnant in 2020 urgently advised by noted Pfizer not to take a Covid vaccine? And above all, why was this advice ignored by all governments? (See also our December 4 article: Pfizer vaccine package insert explicitly warns that "it is unknown whether the Covid vaccine affects fertility.")

With the Covid mRNA vaccines, which intervene directly in our cells by instructing them to produce the spike protein of the SARS-CoV-2 virus, there has been - given the huge number of sick and dead - a new 'assault' on humans. From the occurrence of heart disease, thrombosis, blindness and numerous serious autoimmune diseases, it can be concluded that the genetic instructions have a trigger effect on all sorts of other bodily processes.

You may not notice this initially, but it is not inconceivable that more and more women and girls will find it more difficult to conceive, or that initially apparently healthy children will be born but later turn out to be infertile themselves - exactly as the gene-drive tech aims to do.

While this is still speculation, it is certainly a danger that needs to be looked at very seriously. Indeed, the Covid mRNA vaccines represent a radical departure from the past, as for the first time direct genetic manipulation of humans is being performed, and on an unprecedentedly massive scale at that. If millions of children later turn out to be infertile, we will have destroyed our society and our future - and that for a virus that has proven to be no more dangerous to mankind than a wave of flu. (See also: 11-01: mRNA vaccines: genetic engineering is dangerous because it can cause infertility)

What does Bill Gates really want to achieve?

What does it say that Bill "vaccine" Gates, who in the previous decade financed a remote-controlled implantable contraceptive chip, and who for so long has been propagating the need to significantly reduce the world's population, is a strong proponent of genetic engineering that can be used to exterminate entire (sub)species? As is well known, Gates is one of the main driving forces behind the mass vaccination of the world population against Covid, while time and again it turns out that the least vaccinated countries suffer virtually nothing, and the most vaccinated countries have to contend with the highest disease and mortality rates.

Is this perhaps an indication that there are indeed genetic instructions put into these Covid injections that - just as with an unwanted mosquito population - gradually damage and destroy the health and/or fertility of the recipients, after which possibly the next generation will be much less fertile and therefore far fewer children will be born? In short: the terrifying scenario of "The Handmaid's Tale"?

And then, if this final assault with this eradication technology does indeed take place and succeeds, what will be left of the original humanity after a few generations? As it stands now, possibly only those who have received zero Covid vaccinations will be able to survive - at least, if they also manage to stay out of the hands of the AI/5G/6G global totalitarian control system, which is in the process of being established and in which only a small fraction of humans will be allowed to function as transhuman cyborg slaves (until they are no longer needed).

An ancient prophet once wrote that "mortals will become rarer than purified gold" at a time when the forces of the universe will falter and the earth will "tremble from its place. (Isaiah 13:12). Given all the extremely worrisome developments surrounding vaccinations, an impending Third World War, the rising energy and food crisis, the earth's diminishing magnetic field and the resulting more erratic weather, and a devastating solar flare predicted by astronomers, the moment of fulfillment, now some 2,700 years later, may well be almost upon us.

Latest UK government figures show that birth attendants of all ages do indeed seem to get AIDS

The New England Journal of Medicine (NEJM), considered the leading international medical journal certainly as far as Covid-19 is concerned, sounded the alarm two weeks ago about the safety of the booster shots. In an editorial, Dr. Paul Offit warned that it would further weaken the immune systems of vaccinated people, and increase the risk of ADE (Antibody Dependent Enchancement) reactions.

The latest British government figures confirm this trend predicted by independent scientists, and show that vaccinated people of all ages even appear to be contracting a form of AIDS at a rapid rate. Despite this, British doctors will soon be banned from criticizing the injections.

Dr. Offit initially begins by praising the mRNA injections as obligatory, but then his tone changes completely.

First, he points out that it is unclear exactly which younger age groups would have benefited from the booster shot, because no research has been done on existing medical conditions. The bottom line is that for healthy younger people, the boosters actually make no sense at all.

Then comes a clear warning. Continuing to massively jab boosters because it is falsely believed that this would eliminate Covid, 'will limit the ability of the booster to reduce infections.' The upshot: 'Boosters are not risk-free.

We need to clarify which groups will benefit most. For example, boys and men between the ages of 16 and 29 are at increased risk of myocarditis caused by mRNA vaccines.'

Original Antigenic Sin (= ADE)

'And all age groups are at risk for the theoretical problem of an 'original antigenic sin,' which is a decreased ability to respond to a new immunogen because the immune system has focused on the original immunogen... This potential problem may limit our ability to respond to a new variant.'

The professor of experimental immunology Pierre Capel was one of the first to warn about this 'original antigenic sin', or ADE - Antibody Dependent Enchancement reactions. These arise because vaccine antibodies (against an old, no longer existing variant) in combination with new variants actually strengthen Covid-19, causing vaccinated people to become ill much more quickly and severely than unvaccinated people.

The editorial therefore urges governments to "educate the public about the limitations of mucosal (mRNA Covid) vaccines. Otherwise, a zero tolerance strategy for mild or asymptomatic infections, which can only be achieved with regular booster doses, will continue to mislead the public about what the Covid-19 vaccines can and cannot do.' (Bold added: 'continue' essentially acknowledges that the public has been and continues to be lied to about the safety and effectiveness of these gene-manipulation injections.)

Despite the explosive increase in the number of people with heart disease, thrombosis and other, often serious medical conditions, also in the Netherlands most people continue to repeat the government and media propaganda that the hospitals are (or were) full of unvaccinated people, that side effects and deaths from the injections are 'rare', and that research has shown that the 'vaccines' work so well.

V-AIDS (Vaccine-AIDS)

However, all serious figures and statistics show the opposite. In fact, the latest UK government figures seem to confirm that booster babies do indeed get AIDS, as we have written about in several previous articles. To be precise: V-AIDS, Vaccine-AIDS. (See also our 10-01 article: UK Health Security Agency data point to upcoming mass AIDS outbreak among vaccinated people).

AIDS (Acquired Immunodeficiency Syndrome) is a general term and you definitely don't get it just from the (supposed) HIV virus, as many still seem to think. AIDS involves a step-by-step breakdown of the human immune system, which in time makes even common cold viruses and bacteria life-threatening, and also the natural defenses against other serious diseases such as cancer fail. Immune system failure can also be caused by radiation, chemotherapy, leukemia and malnutrition (especially in Third World countries).

UK statistics are downright devastating for Covid-19 vaccinations and booster shots.

As you can see, precisely boostered people in all age groups are by far the most at risk of getting Covid-19. You may still think that this doesn't say much, because most people have been pricked by now. Nevertheless, these figures clearly show that the injections in no way prevent vaccinated people from becoming infected. Moreover, the following statistic shows that, even in the number of cases per 100,000, boostered people are by far the dominant ones. In fact, the difference between those who are boostered and those who are unvaccinated continues to increase each month.

Vaccins and boosters damage immune system

Medical authorities claim that the effectiveness of vaccines decreases over time and booster shots are therefore necessary, but that is a lie. It is not the strength of the vaccine that declines, but that of the human immune system (compared to that of unvaccinated people). Therefore, an effectiveness of -50% means that the immune system of vaxxers performs a lot worse than that of unvaccinated people, and the Covid-19 shots (and especially the boosters) have thus damaged rather than strengthened that immune system.

By subtracting the number of Covid cases among vaccinated people (per 100,000) from the number of Covid cases among unvaccinated people (per 100,000) and then dividing by the number of cases among vaccinated people x 100.

What you don't know won't hurt you...until

Because of this frightening trend, the UK Health Security Agency (the UK's RIVM) has decided to stop publishing these figures (2). What you don't know won't hurt you... until the immune systems of more and more people who have been born start to fail completely, and they start to become deathly ill even from ordinary household bacteria and viruses, which unvaccinated people don't get or hardly get.

This may not be too bad this spring and summer, but starting in the fall, once the viruses return, the health care system could be overwhelmed, with all the consequences (lockdowns, mouthguards, mandatory injections) that that entails. Indeed, there is no chance that it will be honestly acknowledged that it is not a new variant or different virus, but the injections themselves, that are the cause of so many illnesses and deaths.

Doctors no longer allowed to criticize vaccines and lockdowns

Especially when it is considered that the British General Medical Council (GMC) has new regulations in store that are being portrayed as the 21st century version of Hippocratic Oath. Under these new rules, doctors who criticize vaccines and lockdowns on social media must be removed from the medical register. Doctors must henceforth be "honest" and "trustworthy," and that means no questioning official government policy in the year 2022.

As recently as December 2021, a judge ruled that the GMC had gone too far in accusing and penalizing Dr. Samuel White, who the council said had spread "disinformation" by saying in a video that mouthguards don't help at all (which, by the way, is the proven truth). According to Dr. White, the lies from the government and medical authorities about the pandemic and vaccinations were "so enormous that I can no longer bear them.

Unfortunately, those lies have certainly not diminished - quite the contrary.

Post vaccine damage?

Vaccines change brain, brain, personality and humanity

Dr. Bhakdi: 'We are in the middle of the Apocalypse; humanity is changing, vaccinated people will eventually not be human beings anymore' - *Transport organization US Freedom Flyers: 30% pilots would now not pass medical test because of heart problems due to Covid injections*

German Dr. Sucharit Bhakdi (Doctors for Covid Ethics) gained worldwide fame for being one of the first system scientists to seriously warn people not to take a Covid-19 vaccine. He wrote the notorious bestseller "Corona False Alarm" and its sequel "Corona Unmasked. In a recent interview with Dr. Peter Breggin, Dr. Bhakdi left no doubt: 'I say to everyone who is participating: these (mRNA) vaccines are going to change humanity. They are going to change you - your psyche, your brain. Don't do it. You will lose your individuality and personality. You will no longer be a human being.'

Dr. Bhakdi begins the interview with a poignant message: 'I think we are in the middle of the Apocalypse. The end is near. Everyone MUST understand the danger, and stand up... against this diabolical, satanic, diabological (New World Order) agenda' of the big mega banks, multinational corporations, the military-industrial complex and international organizations like the World Economic Forum.

In the second part of the interview, the scientist explained why, from a scientific point of view, people are easier to manipulate when they have received the mRNA injections. He reiterated the now well-known fact that the Covid shots are not real vaccines, but trigger the human body to produce the toxic spike protein of the (supposed) coronavirus. These spikes, he believes, have only one function: to "open the door" in the cells for the virus.

The damage to the cells that ingest the mRNA is mainly caused by the body's own immune system. This too has already been confirmed in numerous scientific studies. Once the cells start making the spike protein, the immune system will attack these cells and try to kill them. In people suffering from autoimmune diseases, exactly the same thing happens. That means injecting them with mRNA vaccines is tantamount to planting seeds for the emergence of autoimmune diseases.

'Personality people will change'

Indeed, the mRNA 'vaccines' are best compared to 'letters in an envelope,' he continued. These 'letters' travel throughout the body to unknown destinations, and are taken up by cells that the virus would never have reached. These cells are in the lymph nodes and the walls of blood vessels. The damage done to these cells once they receive the 'letters' and carry out the instructions will be enormous; for example, numerous people have already suffered from blood clots (/ brain hemorrhages, thrombosis) and damage to the immune system itself.

'Those who have created these vaccines think they are more than God.

The 'envelope' - consisting of the lipid nanoparticles - is pure poison, as it contains toxic cationic (positively charged) lipids (fat globules). Natural lipids are negatively charged or have no charge at all. Most of the important molecules in our cells are negatively charged. The cationic lipids bind to them and then interfere with their function. These positive lipids can even act directly on the negatively charged DNA, and also on negatively charged proteins necessary for wound healing.

Blood clots are formed wherever blood vessels are damaged. These clots can form in small vessels in places that can never be detected with scans (See also our article of 29-06-21: Professor Bhakdi: 'Research proves that 30% to 40% vaccinated people get blood clots') . Eventually, the clogging of small vessels in the brain will lead to brain damage, which will change people's personalities (either slowly or rapidly).

Pathologists found that 90% deceased people had spikes throughout their bodies

Pfizer and Moderna, according to Dr. Bhakdi, know very well that the damage to these capillaries cannot be easily detected, and think they will get away with it. Pathologists, however, can identify this damage post mortem. For example, last year German pathologists detected the spike protein in all organs, the heart, brain, liver, spleen, lungs and reproductive organs.

Their conclusion was shocking: 90% of people who died after vaccination had symptoms of an autoimmune attack, with the heart as the main target (think of the many hundreds of athletes who suddenly developed heart problems, had to quit or even died).

Numerous studies have shown that it is unpredictable how quickly that process occurs. Some people experience serious problems within days or even hours of their shot; other people can continue to function as if nothing had happened for months after their booster shot and then suddenly become seriously ill and/or die.

At the end of the interview, Dr. Breggin emphasized that "we are at a crucial moment in time. We clearly need people to courageously rise up against these things. About what you heard today: don't become helpless and get upset and overwhelmed. Get angry - but not too angry. Get to work, get active, love. Talk to your neighbors and friends... get active in local politics... Learn as much as you can and be as active as you can. We are now at a point in history where we have to stand up for freedom in the world.

'30% pilots have heart problems because of vaccines'

Another scientist who made a name for himself is cardiologist Dr. Peter McCullough. In an interview on April 20, pilot Joshua Yoder, co-founder of the transportation organization US Freedom Flyers, told tech millionaire Steve Kirsch, founder of the Vaccine Safety Research Foundation, that according to McCullough, 30% of all pilots would not pass the medical test because their hearts were affected by the Covid 'vaccines.

Yoder said that vaccinated pilots have suffered from chest pain, myocarditis and pericarditis. He personally knew at least three pilots who fly with chest pain, and another who is under treatment by a cardiologist.

Recently, American Airlines pilot Robert Snow suffered a heart attack just 6 minutes after landing at the Dallas-Fort Worth airport. He had to be treated with a defibrillator, and was then taken to the hospital. According to Yoder, the Johnson & Johnson vaccine was the culprit. American Airlines, meanwhile, is trying to distance itself as much as possible from the incident.

NEVER take a booster shot, healthcare system will collapse

Virus and vaccine expert Dr. Geert Vanden Bossche, who once worked for the Bill & Melinda Gates Foundation and the GAVI alliance, made it to both international and our national free media with his severe criticism of vaccination policies. In November 2021, he even warned all people to "never take Covid vaccines," because they weaken the human immune system.

Earlier that year, Vanden Bossche warned that providing billions of people with new "vaccines" during a pandemic - an absolute no go in immunology until 2020 - would have dire consequences because it could make the mutations that normally always occur, especially of respiratory viruses like corona, much more dangerous.

He later urged anyone who did get vaccinated not to take a booster shot under any circumstances, because it is "absolutely insane. Booster shots actually put even more pressure on the natural immune system. 'This is dangerous and should not be done.' If boostered people come into contact with all kinds of diseases at some point, what is left of their immune system will have extreme difficulty protecting the body anymore.

Consequently, most vaccinated people, but especially those who are born, will at some point require "intensive medical treatment. At the same time, the immune system of the unvaccinated will actually become more and more powerful. But since the vast majority of people have been vaccinated and boostered, 'this will inevitably lead to the collapse of our healthcare system. I'm not a doomsday preacher, but it can't be said any other way.'

Chemtrail craziness?

Climate interventions pose danger to people, ecosystems and geopolitical stability - *Just the WEF warned in 2013 that chemtrails can cause drought -* ***Possible link between chemtrails and vaccine activation discussed as early as 2010***

Chemtrails were invariably laughed off in the past as a conspiracy theory of 'geeks', but have now been a recognized and established fact for many years. Solar Radiation Management' (SRM) is the official name for the spraying into the atmosphere of all kinds of potentially harmful chemicals that are supposed to reflect sunlight in order to reduce 'Global Warming' (and this at a time when a period of Global Cooling has just begun). Nature Communications has now published a university study in which scientists warn that, as a result of SRM (chemtrails), 1 billion more people are at risk of contracting malaria.

Geoengineering, or "messing around" with the climate, has never proven to be a good idea, but nevertheless is being tried again and again. The United Arab Emirates, for example, has been using cloud seeding technology for several years, spraying salt and chemicals into clouds ("chemtrails") to promote precipitation. Drones are also used to deliver electric shocks to clouds, causing them to release their moisture and start raining. There is then a risk of causing 'flash floods', flooding and landslides.

Chemtrails recognized and discussed at climate conferences as early as 2010

Serious proposals to (continue to) spray aluminum and barium into the atmosphere to block sunlight were already discussed at the international climate conference in Cancun in 2010. 'Chemtrails' had been around for a while as a 'conspiracy theory' at the time, and were actually officially recognized at that point.

Aluminum was considered harmless until recently, but now it can be found in almost everything (soil, food, water, cosmetics, medicine, vaccines). It builds up in the human body for years, and then can cause substantial health problems (Parkinson's, Alzheimer's, fatigue, possibly even cancer, as well as memory and concentration and behavior problems in children).

Breathing air containing barium compounds can lead to so-called 'dust lungs'. Barium (compound) soluble in moisture (rainwater?) is toxic and can interfere with both breathing and heart rhythm, increase blood pressure, cause brain swelling and damage liver, heart and kidneys.

Also at the 10th UN Biodiversity Convention conference in Nagoya, Japan, in 2010, the existence of chemtrails was almost explicitly admitted with the decision to actually ban countries from further experimenting with spraying chemicals into the atmosphere. Incidentally, no country seems to have taken any notice of that ban.

A recent test planned in Sweden by Bill 'vaccine' Gates to dim the sun by releasing calcium carbonate particles into the atmosphere was cancelled after much protest. 'You can't test the detonator of a bomb and then say this can't possibly hurt,' responded Niclas Hällström, director of the 'green' Swedish think tank WhatNext?

1 billion more people at risk of malaria

Scientists from Georgetown University Medical Center and others are warning that large-scale use of SRM ("chemtrails"), such as injecting aerosols into the stratosphere that are supposed to reflect sunlight, could have very undesirable consequences because it could promote dangerous infectious diseases such as malaria.

Eight researchers from the US, Bangladesh, Germany and South Africa used various climate models to simulate what could happen if geoengineering were used to reduce 'Global Warming'. The models calculated with temperatures most conducive to the Anopheles mosquito, and also with the number of people living in areas where they could be infected.

In both the medium and high warming scenarios, it turns out that the risk of malaria shifts significantly from region to region. In the highest scenario, an additional 1 billion people will be at risk of malaria as a result of geoengineering (chemtrails). 'On a planet that is too warm for humans, it also becomes too warm for the malaria parasite,' explained Colin Carlson, assistant research professor at the Center for Global Health

Science and Security. 'Cooling the planet could be an emergency measure to save lives, but it would also work the opposite way.'

Danger to people, ecosystems and geopolitical stability

Malaria infection peaks at 25 degrees Celsius. Cooling the tropics with chemtrails could increase the risk of malaria not only in the future, but also now. 'That geoengineering could reduce the danger of climate change remains poorly understood. It could create a range of new risks to people and ecosystems,' warned Christopher Trisos, senior researcher at the University of Cape Town.

The most startling finding of the study was that geoengineering will be able to significantly reduce the risk of malaria especially in the Indian subcontinent, but will actually increase the risks in Southeast Asia (1). This fact alone makes the decision to proceed with climate interventions geopolitically complex and also dangerous. Indeed, countries that will be heavily affected by these interventions could well react aggressively.

WEF warned in 2013 of drought caused by chemtrails

In 2013, the now highly controversial World Economic Forum, of all places, warned in its annual risk report about the uncontrolled use of geoengineering, such as blocking sunlight by spraying chemical particles into the atmosphere, because this method 'can inadvertently cause drought' (think back to some very hot and dry summers in recent years). 'The global climate could be 'hijacked' in this way by a rogue state or even a stone-age individual, with unpredictable costs to agriculture, infrastructure and global stability.' (2)

Drought caused by chemtrails was characterized 9 years ago as one of five 'X-Factor' problems for the world. The four others?

1) Out-of-control climate change;
2) Magnetic stimulation of our brains; (were 5G/nanobots planned back then?)

3) Unsustainable medical costs due to extended life spans; (hence depopulation by injections?)

4) The discovery of extraterrestrial life and the implications for humanity. (No joke!)

Link between chemtrails and vaccinations?

In our article, 'Sinister link between chemtrails and swine flu vaccinations' (December 21, 2010), we cited an unnamed insider from the largest investment bank on Wall Street, who allegedly said that the injections against swine and bird flu were not real vaccinations, but 'the introduction of a protein that is one component of a virus.'

'It works almost the same way as the AIDS virus: its main function is to remain 'dormant' until it is activated

by, say, an attack with biological weapons (or
chemtrails. That 'attack' can also be a follow-up
'vaccination', such as a booster shot). Thus, the people
who receive these vaccinations are in effect accepting a
protein that actually infects them with a virus. This part
remains inactive until the activating component - or
protein linked DNA - enters the body.'

Also at the time, a senior EPA official (Environmental
Protection Agency) is said to have revealed just before
his death that a man-made virus would be released in
the future that would terrify the entire population.
Because of that fear, people would willingly (and
eagerly) accept a mandatory "vaccine. Some time after
administration, a second component would then indeed
be added (e.g., by chemtrails and/or booster shots),
creating a lethal combination.

Well, if you have followed the reports on free media
such as this site, and also look at the frightening
statistics of the sharply increasing number of deaths
and serious health problems, you probably don't need
any further explanation that there are many indications
that this is exactly what could be done with the Covid-
19 mRNA gene manipulation injections. (The swine flu
quickly turned out to be a storm in a teacup, after which
millions of 'vaccines' had to be discarded unused, This
'pandemic' therefore seems to have been a kind of
dress rehearsal).

Covid total control?

Biodigital Convergence: Governments actively working toward full integration human with digital entities

----

The now infamous futurist and WEF speaker Yuval Noah Harari, professor of history at the Hebrew University of Jerusalem and top advisor to Klaus Schwab, is winding down and acknowledging that Covid-19 is being used to put everyone "under the skin under total biometric surveillance. This means that the mandatory introduction of implanted/injected nanochips is now well and truly upon us, and the digital aspect of the 'Mark of the Beast' will be a fait accompli within a few years. We suspect that many vaccinated people, whose bodies have already been injected with mRNA nanotech via the Covid 'vaccines', have now been brainwashed to such an extent that they will eagerly queue up for that chip. Fine, they'll know right away if I'm infected!"

Covid is crucial, because it convinces people to accept and acknowledge total biometric control. If we want to stop this epidemic, we have to monitor not just people, but what's going on under their skin.' 'That's what governments want to know: what's our body temperature? Our blood pressure? Our medical condition (or vaccination status)?'

Some of Harari's well-known earlier statements:

In an interview with 60 Minutes, he once said that 'so far we've seen companies and governments collecting data on where we go, who we meet, and what movies we watch. In the next phase, control will go under our skin.'

'People are gaining greater power than ever. We develop actual divine powers of creation and destruction. We upgrade humans to gods, and gain the power to redesign life.... Humans are now hackable animals (CNN inverview November 2019). The whole idea that people have a soul or spirit, that they have free will and nobody knows what's going on inside them, that they have free will to make a choice, whether it's for the election or at the supermarket, is over.'

'Data is worth much more in the world today than money. Ten years ago, big companies were paying billions for WhatsApp and In-stagram, and people wondered if they were crazy. The reason? Because they were producing data. Increasingly, the world is being more or less split into spheres of data collection and collation. In the Cold War, you had the Iron Curtain. Now we have the Silicon Curtain between the US and China: where does the data go? California, or to Shenzhen, Shanghai and Beijing?'

Biodigital convergence

In 2020, Policy Horizons, a strategic organization within Canadian government, published the report 'Exploring

Biodigital Convergence', which stated that already in the near future 'biology and digital technology' will merge, and a new kind of (transhuman) human will emerge. On that subject, once 'science fiction' but now becoming reality, we have written extensively in recent years.

'It is more than a technological change. This biodigital convergence (fusion) may transform the way we understand ourselves, and cause us to redefine what we consider human or natural... Digital technologies and biological systems are beginning to unite and merge with each other in ways that may deeply disrupt our assumptions about society, the economy and our bodies. We call this the biodigital convergence. Which opens up amazing new ways to change human beings - our bodies, minds and behaviors... (And) to change or create other organisms.'

For those who still don't want to believe what was and/or may have been put into the Covid-19 injections, 'Digital technology can be embedded in organisms, and biological components can exist as parts of digital technologies.

The physical mixing, manipulation, and confluence of the biological and the digital create new hybrid life forms and new technology, each functioning with often enhanced capabilities in the tangible world.'

Brain interfaces and neural implants

For example, robots with biological brains and biological bodies with digital brains already exist, as do human-computer and brain-machine interfaces. Digitally manipulated insects such as drone dragonflies and "surveillance" grasshoppers are examples of this merging of bio with digi-tech. By tapping into our nervous system, neurons can be manipulated, and tech can be added to change the function and purpose of an organism. For example, scientists have already equipped rat brains with many additional "wires" that can be used to deliver information and commands to the brain.

People are given digital interfaces in (/ to) their brains, with which they can give thought commands to, for example, open an app that, via injected nanotech, monitors and, if necessary, adjusts the health of the body. In this way, contact could also be made with the Internet, which will then have evolved into the Metaverse (/Metaversum), to which in time many will presumably remain almost chronically linked. The interface also records your dreams, allowing you to look back and analyze them later. It also allows you to program your dreams.

In short: the classical concept of what 'life' is, will in fact disappear. Life will no longer be purely biological, but also - and in the long run perhaps especially and even totally - technological. For some this may sound fantastic, but don't forget that neural and other physical implants and (nano)tech will be under constant external A.I. 5G/6G control, and you really won't have any freedom or privacy anymore, so also - as Harari said - you won't have any freedom of choice or free will.

Most people happy with android slave status

People will even be able to be programmed to be perfectly happy with their android slave status. Any memory of what it was once like to be a natural, free and independent human being will be stopped and erased.

Personally, it seems to me an abomination of the worst order, but for many people who actually find life too difficult and complicated, handing over all responsibilities may be music to their ears.

When I look at how thoughtlessly and mindlessly the vast majority of the population agreed to the most absurd and pernicious corona measures from 2020 onwards, and then to now highly harmful experimental mRNA gene manipulation injections, I fear that this may well be true for the vast majority. And that, of course, is exactly what the WEF elite are all about ("You'll own nothing and be happy").

WEF announced digital 'sign of the Beast' almost literally in February

On February 20, we paid attention to the new WEF report Advancing Towards Digital Agency, which almost literally announced a digital 'sign of the Beast' system. The bottom line is that everyone is going to have some kind of personal digital 'god' who is going to make all the important decisions for you, because based on all your personal data, that 'god' would know exactly what you want and need, and when and where. And 'of course' the government is going to totally control ANY aspect of this process, this 'god', and therefore YOU.

This digital profile 'may contain inherent data characteristics (such as biometrics)(= physical characteristics), or assigned characteristics (such as names or national ID numbers)'.

Once this digital ID, which will be embedded in your body in the next phase, is in place and embedded, it will also include your purchasing behavior and medical situation, plus your 'assessments and decisions' based on your profile and social/financial behavior ('a bank decides the attractiveness of an individual for a loan'). This is nothing less than the social credit system as rolled out in China.

Integrating transhuman humans with global control system

The use of (eventually mandatory) 'vaccinations' with advanced (nano) tech to build the 'sign of the Beast' system IN your body, so that you will surrender your free will in ALL areas and will no longer be able to resist this A.I. 'god' in the making, we predicted back in 2009. (See also our article of 03-09: 'Implantable 5G nanotech biosensor already as of 2021 in Covid-19 vaccines' (/

Transhuman being integrated with global digital control system)).

There will be no escape from that system, not only because it is deliberately designed as a kind of eternal prison and because these gene therapy injections will have irreversible health consequences for many anyway, but also because you will become an inseparable part of that technocratic 'Beast' system, in which you will be 'online' every second of the day to follow, control, steer, modify and change.

Just as you cannot remove the mRNA nanotech and spikes of the Covid 'vaccines' from your body, you will find it impossible to remove yourself from 'the Beast' because you have 'fused' with it. Indeed, you will no longer be an original 'human', but will have been transformed into a transhuman android, a kind of 'cyborg'. Then you will be worshipped by a digital 'god' forever, a cyborg god: the A.I. of Schwab's 'Internet of Bodies', the digital personification of Lucifer (/ Satan) on Earth.

Do we live in a simulation?

Awareness key to escape from the Matrix: Humans limit their own power. *If they did exercise it, we could transcend this reality and "rewrite our own history*

The legendary science fiction trilogy The Matrix (Part 1 in 1999) depicted how hyper-intelligent technological beings, controlled by an 'omnipotent' A.I., keep humanity trapped in a kind of dream world. Hacker Thomas Anderson (aka 'Neo') discovers that the reality around him is not real, but a digital holographic illusion intended to keep all people under control, and especially unaware of the existence of this 'Matrix'. While most people associate this concept with 'fantasy' precisely because of these films, science appears to be getting closer and closer to proving that we are indeed living in some kind of externally controlled 'Matrix', and reality is completely different than humanity has always thought.

A research paper from the University of Portsmouth (England) has published an experiment that seems to confirm that there is a 'fifth state of matter', say a 'fifth element' in the universe: information. Dr. Melvin Vopson published in the journal AIP Advances his findings that information has mass, and that all elementary particles (the smallest building blocks of the universe) have information stored about themselves, just as humans have in their DNA.

If the experiment is proven correct, Vopson will have discovered that in addition to solid, liquid, gas and plasma, there is a fifth state of matter: information. 'This would be a eureka moment, because it would change physics as we know it, and broaden our understanding of the universe,' he commented. 'And it doesn't contradict quantum mechanics, electrodynamics, thermodynamics, or classical mechanics. It completes physics with something new and unimaginably exciting.'

At least one-third universe may be made up of information

According to Vopson, the mysterious "dark matter," which makes up nearly one-third of the universe, could be made up of information. 'If we assume that information is material and has mass, and that elementary particles have a DNA of information about themselves, how can we prove it? My latest paper tests these theories so that they can be taken seriously by the scientific community.'

This information, he says, can be proven by colliding particles with anti-particles (as is done in the Large Hadron Collider, for example). If particles then mutually annihilate each other, the information from these particles is converted into low-energy infrared photons.

Now that all particles (visible and invisible) seem to consist partly of information, the well-known 'The Matrix' image (green numbers sliding vertically at lightning speed across a black screen, and later in the movies the whole world that appears to be built from this) suddenly becomes a lot more understandable and likely.

Simulation hypothesis supported by scientists

In his book 'The Simulation Hypothesis' (2019), Professor Rizwan Virk, (Massachusetts Institute of Technology / MIT) listed a number of strong arguments that challenged our physical world. 'I would say that the probability of us living in a simulation is somewhere between 50% and 100%. I think it's more likely that we are in a simulation than not,' he stated in an interview with Digital Trends.

Virk was certainly not the first to bring up the 'Matrix' concept (albeit not literally). Back in 2003, Oxford professor Nick Bostrom wrote the article, "Are you living in a simulation? In it, he made a mathematically based case for the simulation hypothesis. A civilization with sufficient computer power could succeed in allowing people to live (or be imprisoned) in new digital 'worlds'. Over time, those people might forget that the world around them is not real, but merely a digital hologram, a simulation.

Tesla, SpaceX, Neuralink (and now Twitter) owner Elon Musk is one of the high-profile figures who also believes in the reality of a "Matrix. In 2018, during a popular podcast broadcast, he said that "video games will eventually be indistinguishable from reality. We are most likely in a simulation.'

Consciousness key to escape from the Matrix

This is also the starting point in the book by Dutch investigative journalist Martin Vrijland. If we assume that we live (observe/play) in a simulation, then our human body is a kind of avatar in a Playstation game... It is therefore essential to realize that you are not your body, but through your body you are an observer in this simulation. Your consciousness is, as it were, looking through your body into this simulation.'

By the way, the American investigative journalist Jon Rappoport wrote about this 'Matrix' already at the beginning of this century. In his three books (The Matrix Revealed, Exit From the Matrix and Power Outside The Matrix) he reveals the key to escaping the false reality of the Matrix: imagination. Or, in other words, consciousness.

'No matter how you look at it, 99.99999999% of the "spiritual systems" of this world revolve around denying individual power. In the end, they all claim that this power comes from another place (an external 'God' etc.). Modern science is no better; it defines mind as the brain, and nothing more. Moreover, people limit their own power, which, if exercised, would transcend reality.'

Indeed, with our consciousness we are able to create a new reality, one that is not only separate from the current Matrix prison, but can defeat it. Only then can a true new world finally be created that is many times better and more just.

'Humanity can rewrite its own history'

Humanity itself studies and observes its own world. Within a participatory universe, man creates her own reality by focusing her gaze and consciously investigating the world for the world she desires,' writes Dutch author Helma Broekman on her unique channel. 'This is the true act of Creation. EVERYWHERE the human being consciously looks at, consciously feels and consciously perceives, the consciousness makes something to look at.'

'The INTENTION, LOVE and EXPECTATION that something exists may yet be precisely the POWER of our Consciousness, which creates a visible New and Lovelier world. Could this be the reason that Humanity needs to be eradicated? The darkness wants to prevent at all costs?'

'By directing your Pure Consciousness with a Loving Free Gaze at the world around you, it could still be possible that this Loving Consciousness with freedom for all, forms the actual act of creation for this New Consciousness... And then Mankind itself (re)writes its loving history!' concludes Broekman.

Science fiction has become fact: we are in a prequel to The Matrix.

'Science fiction has become fact,' John Whitehead wrote for the Rutherford Institute in 2019. 'We are living in a prequel to The Matrix, falling further by the day under the spell of technology-driven worlds, virtual realities, and conveniences controlled by machines with artificial intelligence, which are rapidly working to replace and ultimately dominate us in every area of our lives.'

''We have become slaves to it,'' Whitehead continued. ''Just look around you: everywhere you see people so addicted to their Internet-connected screens that they can spend hours immersed in a virtual world where human interaction is filtered through the medium of technology.''

'This is not freedom. This is not even progress. This is a technological tyranny with the iron fist of a control state, of giants such as Google and Facebook and government spy agencies...' They have created a virtual world with the idea that we still live in a democracy and have a parliament that represents the people, when in reality we are 'little more than slaves to an authoritarian regime, which constantly controls us and presents us with spectacle through the media', meanwhile reversing the law and trying to silence any opposition in ever harsher and more authoritarian ways.

'It is not only our freedom that is at stake, but humanity itself,' Whitehead believes. Google, which through its global ramifications is already a neural network that functions as a 'world brain', is developing so rapidly that the moment at which this network knows everything about you because it has stored and analyzed every email, every document and every search is getting ever closer. And through Google, even the intelligence services may know more about you than you do.

Technocratic tyranny 2030 in the making

Technological developments are now moving so fast that futurist Ray Kurzweil's year of the 'singularity', the year in which transhuman humanity merges into a The Matrix-like virtual world simulation - now better known as the 'Metaverse' - is being pushed further and further forward. The original target year of 2050 has now become 2030, and according to some the first people will probably be able to connect to the Metaverse years earlier. Around 2030 there could then be an actual 'uploading' of consciousness.

3 years ago I concluded an article on this topic as follows (some words modified): The only thing that could still stop this technocratic tyranny is a mass awakening, a mass consciousness, culminating in a definitive break with the Luciferian simulation (the Matrix) that keeps us prisoner, and that wants to push us between now and 2030 into an eternal digital slavery from which escape is definitively impossible.'

Since then, the necessary people have woken up, but there is still too little real awareness of this. Moreover, the time for this seems to be getting shorter and shorter.

A techno-dimensional war?

In the end times, two groups of people are spiritually 'sealed' on/behind their foreheads - *Many Christians and churches infected with demons*

Our series 'Forbidden Gates: The Beginning of the Techno Dimensional War' in 2010 was considered by many at the time to be pure science fiction, something for that would be far in the future. Please read in this second updated volume (originally published on September 5, 2010) that what seemed like fantasy at the time has now become harsh, lurid reality. DMT (Dimethyltryptamine), an Amazonian drug, has rapidly conquered the West over the past 10 years. In the U.S. at the time, "DMT churches" where people ritually sought contact with spirits were springing up like mushrooms. Banned in the Netherlands, DMT is a very powerful psychoactive drug that drags the user into the spirit world within seconds of ingestion. The best known drug containing DMT is ayahuasca.

The chemical DMT is produced in small quantities naturally by the epiphysis (pineal gland) in our own brains. This gland is located behind the forehead and is sometimes called the "third eye" by biologists and spiritualists, because the gland contains biological elements similar to the retina of our eyes. Animals with an epiphysis actually use this gland as an internal organ of perception.

An areligious journalist from the renowned magazine National Geographic traveled to the Amazon jungle to investigate the effects of DMT, which has been found there for thousands of years in wild plants and used by indigenous shamans to contact spirits. Part of a "sacred circle," the woman ingested a traditional cup of Ayahuasca tea (containing DMT), after which she says she almost immediately seemed to fall into an abyss, where she allegedly heard cries from doomed souls begging for them to be released.

She then found herself in a hellscape in front of three dark thrones, and heard threatening voices telling her that she would never get out of there and that there was no hope for her. She was "saved" by the other participants of the "sacred circle," who had also taken DMT. It is common for the participants of such a circle to see the same apparitions, such as snakes twisting around them.

Scientific research proves spiritual effect of DMT

Of note is an official clinical study on the effects of DMT, which was conducted by psychologist Dr. Rick Strassman, affiliated with the University of New Mexico (USA). He published the results of his scientific research in his book 'DMT: The Mind Molecule'. He discovered that test subjects who took DMT had spiritual experiences within seconds that most resembled so-called "alien abductions. These subjects had been selected in advance and did not know or care about these UFO/alien stories.

The beings that many DMT users encountered were described as the familiar 'greys', reptilian or insect-like creatures. The contact usually consisted of medical and reproductive experiments -described as violent rapes- performed by these entities on the subjects. Remarkably, if these test subjects were willing to take DMT again later, they reported afterwards that the beings with whom they were in contact again were aware of their earlier 'disappearance', but with no awareness of loss of time.

The experiences of the various spirit world 'journeys' were so traumatic for these clinical subjects that a support group was later formed to help them cope with the emotional trauma they had suffered as a result of the encounters with these beings.

Others who use DMT also describe a different kind of reality, but one full of light and love, a place where they get in touch with intelligent beings. But whether the experience is positive or negative, the impact of a DMT "trip" on the emotional, mental and spiritual state of each user is enormous, casting doubt on the stability and judgment of those who take these types of "trips" multiple times.

According to Dr. J. Michael Bennett, it is quite possible that the pineal gland in our brains is an organ through which contact can be made with the spiritual world. Ancient records show that so-called "fallen angels" who visited the Earth taught humans about the use of plants and other natural substances for ritual "magic" and other ceremonies. This may have included the use of DMT derived from wild plants. An "overdose" of DMT can deactivate the neutralizing effect that our stomach naturally has on this chemical.

Two groups of people sealed

It is noteworthy that in the apocalyptic book of Revelation, the 'forehead' is also mentioned, the area of our pineal gland, where people receive a 'seal' that is either from God or Lucifer/satan, protecting one group of sealed people from the influence and effects of the other group. Example: in Revelation 7, 144,000 chosen people are sealed at their foreheads, making them the only ones who are invulnerable to the demonic torments that will appear on Earth from the 'pit of the abyss' (= presumably another dimension) in the (now begun) end times; either as separate beings, or as spiritual entities IN humans, who have been made specially receptive and vulnerable to them through the Covid injections.

Theologians generally consider the number of only 144,000 chosen people to be symbolic. Nevertheless, given the very small number of fully conscious (i.e., really awake) people, the question can gradually be asked whether these 144,000 might (also) represent a literal number.

As a counter-image, Satan seals the foreheads of all his followers by means of 'the Beast' with a 'sign'. Anyone who accepts and receives this sign will be forever damned under eternal judgment (Rev. 19). In addition, we read that at the end of the battle, God will affix his own seal to the forehead of everyone who is saved, with his own name written on it (Rev. 22).

Usually it is assumed that in both cases it is an invisible, spiritual 'sign' directly related to the spiritual (consciousness) state of man. Some interpreters think that in the case of the sign of the Beast it also concerns a visible and/or physical 'sign', such as nanochips implanted or injected via vaccines and other (partly graphene oxide-based) tech.

Mandalas and a One-Parent Strive

Using a psychoactive drug like DMT is certainly not the only way to open the "gates" to the spirit world. Leading New Ager Robert Hieronimus sees the circular design and associated symbolism of the Great Seal of the USA as an "initiatory mandala" that can put the subconscious in touch with the spiritual dimension.

Spiritists and occultists often use these mandalas-the Hindu term for "circles"-as a "protective medium," through which they say they can open and close "gates" to supernatural reality, and allegedly summon or restrain certain entities. The big question, of course, is whether such entities would indeed be stopped by this, and might actually gain power and access through it.

Another way in which immaterial spirits from "the other side" can influence our world is if people consciously or unconsciously pursue the same goals as these beings. Demonologists agree that powerful non-human energies can result from such a one-parent pursuit of power and influence, especially if this pursuit is sanctioned by certain rituals and sacrifices that empower the Dark. The reverse is just as true: a powerful one-parent pursuit based on love and solidarity will be supported by the Divine flow of Light.

The Nazis and the possession of Adolf Hitler

It is widely believed in esoteric circles that the Nazis were a prime example of the Dark pursuit. Their goals and actions were the visible results of the workings of invisible forces with which they had allied themselves. During the rise of Nazi Germany, Hermann Rauschning, the governor of Danzig (the present city of Gdansk in Poland), described how Adolf Hitler "wakes up in the middle of the night screaming and convulsing. He cries out for help, seems half paralyzed and overcome by panic, and shakes so violently that the bed shakes. He makes confused and incomprehensible noises and gasps for breath as if he is about to suffocate.

Rauschning also reported a strange incident in which Hitler -who, according to the Vatican's chief exorcist, Father Gabriele Amorth, who died in 2016, was possessed by the devil himself- was visited by an invisible being whom he was terrified of, and who he knew had come to 'get' him because of the countless innocent victims he had made:

'Hitler stood swaying in his room, looking all around him, as if he had lost his way. 'It's him, it's him!' he groaned. 'He has come for me!' His lips were white and he was perspiring heavily. Suddenly he vomited out a series of meaningless sounds, and then words and parts of sentences. It was terrifying. He used strange expressions connected in bizarre disorder. Then he became silent again, but his lips were still moving. Then suddenly, stamping his feet, he shouted, 'There, there, in the corner! He's there! After he was assured that there was nothing there, they managed to quiet him down again.'

Tainted with demons

Despite such terrifying testimonies, millions of people all over the world are curious about opening the "gates" to the spirit world and making contact with the beings that reside there. This even includes a whole generation of "Christians". In numerous countries the use of occultism (such as casting curses on each other) is the order of the day. (Given the current events, it is worth noting that one of the most occult countries in this regard is Ukraine.)

About 20 years ago, "pastors" and "preachers" appeared in the evangelical world who practiced a new form of "necromancy," talking and having contact with spirits (of the dead). One of the best known is Benny

Hinn, who wrote as early as the 1990s about, among other things, encounters with the deceased Kathryn Kuhlman, at whose grave he says he charges his 'anointing'. In American evangelical churches, things like spirit summoning, levitation, and rituals in which believers sit in circles and imitate animal noises were (and still are) seen.

Even the well-known 'falling in spirit', a phenomenon practiced in evangelical and Pentecostal churches for decades, is in reality a contamination (and sometimes even occupation) with 'Kundalini' demons posing as the Light (the Spirit of God). After 'falling', 'laughing', 'crying' and 'freezing' in the spirit, there were even reports and images of 'puking in the spirit' and 'holy vomit' (things that incidentally also occur during ayahuasca ceremonies). As early as the 1990s, this kind of mind-boggling business (and even open urination) was observed at the bizarre services of the controversial Nigerian Pentecostal 'prophet' T.B. Joshua, who died last year at the age of 57, according to numerous rumors shortly after having a Covid-19 vaccine injected.

In fact, Christian pastors, elders and pastoral staff who believe they have "spiritual insight" and claim to be experts on the spiritual world and on demons actually accomplish the opposite with their "deliverance ministry," namely, making people bound to the influence of dark beings from the spiritual world. According to witnesses, there are even churches, especially in the U.S., that deliberately allow evil spirits to 'temporarily' take possession of the believers during normal services in order to obtain information and messages from 'the other side'. Often these types of church leaders consider themselves very 'special' and refuse to be corrected by anyone.

Especially in Christian churches where people claim to have the only correct spiritual discernment, the work of the Dark is more often than not attributed to the Light. In fact, however, this has been true since the establishment of the false Christian system religion by the Roman Emperor Constantine in the 4th century. The Vatican, with its false light message, can therefore be described as by far the largest, most powerful, and most dangerous demonic sect ever.

Parallel universes?

Existence and workings of parallel earth explained in detail in book 'New Dawn II' (2017) - *Who controls this 'shadow' creation? How do you avoid being trapped in it forever?*

Several media outlets reported on a NASA statement that 'something strange' was going on with the universe. They remained remarkably vague about exactly what that 'something strange' was; it would have something to do with the universe expanding faster than expected. In journals, however, astrophysicists and other scientists are much more specific about what the new discoveries could mean. And then it is not so strange that it is not publicized, because in fact they have found the first evidence for the existence of an invisible "mirror world" that looks almost exactly like ours.

Reality is many times more complex than assumed until recently, as new scientific research has certainly shown in recent years. Especially in recent months we have regularly paid attention to ideas, theories and concepts that most people still refer to as fables, but which turn out to make a lot of sense. In fact, it is precisely the classical image of reality, which is mainly based solely on visual perception and archaic religious interpretations of both the material and the invisible world, that is increasingly proving to be seriously outdated.

'Ghostly mirror world'

A "ghostly mirror world" may well be the reason for the "cosmic controversy" brought out by NASA, writes Steve Can of the University of New Mexico. New research suggests that there is an invisible "mirror world" of particles that interact with us only through gravity. This explanation may be the solution to the major issue that the speed at which the universe is expanding is much greater than predicted by the Hubble constant within the cosmological standard model.

Francis-Yan Cyr-Racine, ass.professor of department of physics and astronomy at the University of New Mexico, Fei Ge and Lloyd Knox of the University of California think they have found a solution for fitting the faster expansion within the accepted cosmological models and constants, without completely overturning them. In doing so, they argue that there is an "inherent symmetry" in many observations once the universe is viewed and studied as one cosmological whole (a kind of holistic approach to the universe, i.e.).

Our world a copy of the original?

In their research paper "Symmetry of Cosmological Observables, a Mirror World Dark Sector, and the Hubble Constant," recently published in Physical Review Letters, the researchers write that if the universe somehow uses this symmetry, there must exist a mirror universe that looks almost exactly like ours. This mirror universe is invisible and unmeasurable, except for the gravitational impact it has on our world.

Cyr-Racine even literally talks about a "parallel universe with new particles that are all copies of known particles. The idea that parallel-or mirror-worlds and universes exist has been prevalent in science fiction books and movies for decades, and was first seriously considered in science in the 1990s. Nevertheless, it was not previously considered as a possible solution to the problem of the Hubble constant.

There can hardly be any question of a data or calculation error anymore, given the multitude of measurements, all of which provide a consistent picture. Moreover, "there is a lot of physics literature on such mirror worlds, but in a completely different context, because they can help explain major problems in particle physics. (1) Again, these are clear indications that the existence of such a mirror universe, as fantastic as it sounds, is real.

By the way, it could just as well be the other way around, namely that our universe and our world consist of almost exact copies of (particles of) the invisible original universe. In other words, that we live in a copy of the original - a copy that is almost the same, but in one small, but very crucial part is still significantly different and functions differently.

Two creations and a parallel earth

Lately we have been paying regular attention to the Dutch author Helma Broekman, whose sensational books and articles may at first seem like science fiction, but for which more and more scientific evidence is emerging. This is also the case now; the existence of a 'mirror world' or 'mirror universe' she has described in detail numerous times.

In her book 'New Dawn II' it is extensively explained that there are two 'creations', 'a world of Light and Omnipresence. The AL, where time, space and form do not exist. And a world of creation, a smaller (Whole) AL, which works with time, space, dimensions and (life) forms (p.12).'

The earth we are on is 'a copy of a much lower frequency and power than the new real earth... On the parallel original earth, however, all life is present without controlled programs. It is a world based on life, not death and impermanence. The parallel earth is the world of Light and being connected to the AL Consciousness... It is this world, where the lion sleeps with the lamb...' (pp. 117-118).

However, here we live in a 'holographic copy of the original earth', on which runs a 'program' that keeps us cut off from the original, and which is used by beings ('gods') as a playing field to manipulate and imprison humanity, and thus maintain and expand the Demiurgic creation.

Not God, but the Demiurge controls this 'shadow' creation

In her 54th video ('Digital Avatar growing faster than Human Consciousness' - see bottom of this article), Broekman explains, from about the 23rd minute, in razor-sharp detail how the creation we have been placed in is controlled, manipulated and executed not by the true God, but by this Demiurge. (This Gnostic principle is essentially the answer to the ever-gnawing question of Christians in particular as to why an "all-powerful and all-knowing God" allows so much misery in this world. There are always theologically correct answers to that, but in my experience they satisfy almost no one).

'The Demiurge has copied from the original field (the original creation) 99.9% of that original field, but that 0.1% just barely. Because that belongs to God, that is to the Light itself, to the original field itself. That means that all His creations, including us, are 99.9% divine, but 0.1% is not yet finished, is half work ('Demiurge' = 'half work').

'Because this last piece is just not finished, it is therefore possible to capture on that one piece your consciousness, and place it in an artificial field, with an artificial time within the space of the original field. And THAT is the Matrix' (See also our article: 01-05: More evidence of the Matrix: Information seems to be fifth element of the universe). We are held on that one (Demiurgic) piece within framed time/space

107

coordinates. Our consciousness then goes on to live only on that 0.1%.

Avoid being trapped in the Metaverse forever

'I think it's about time that humanity accepts and gets clear that what you see with your life and your body in the ether is an almost perfect form, and is exactly the same as what you see here on earth... which is actually reality, a small part of which is manifest' in our 3D world, Broekman said. 'Reality in fact takes place in the ether, in the astral field. And from the ether, parts of energy become manifest on the earth.'

Of course, science will never literally adopt such a spiritual explanation, so it will stick to technical and abstract terms. But I underlined the last conclusion anyway, because it actually describes exactly what the scientific research of Cyr-Racine, Ge and Knox suggests, namely the existence of another world/reality, a 'mirror reality', which acts on us via energetic forces.

The soon-to-be-constructed Metaverse, in which a digital avatar of everyone must be created, is intended to keep all humans permanently imprisoned in this shadow creation of the Demiurge, of Lucifer, that is. For in the Metaverse you will no longer be aware of your own thoughts and your biological system. This 'eternal' imprisonment must be prevented at all costs, and that begins with yourself, by turning inwards and purifying yourself, so that the Demiurge / Lucifer (and the elite) will not have the chance to lock you up forever.

'So look at where your trigger point is, and avoid bringing out any more residual energy.' Broekman concludes with a seldom heard, but oh so important warning: 'If humanity doesn't do its homework, the Light can't just say: well, here's Noah's boat, step on it and I'll take you to safety. It doesn't work that way. We need to work on our boat ourselves, to build our inner 'boat of Noah' together.'